Betty Crocker's

SOUPS AND STEWS COOKBOOK

 GOLDEN PRESS/NEW YORK

Western Publishing Company, Inc.
Racine, Wisconsin

Editor: Bonita Machel
Publishing Coordinator: Shelagh Canning
Publishing Consultant: Carol Paradis
Photography Advisor: Elizabeth Lemmer
Food Styling Coordinator: Mary Sethre
Food Stylists: Carol Grones, Cindy Lund,
             Maria Rolandelli, Linel Polesky
Art Director: Remo Cosentino
Designer: Diane Wagner
Photographer: Steven Smith
Illustrator: Stan Skardinski

First Printing This Format, 1986

Printed in U.S.A. by Western Publishing Company, Inc.
Published by Golden Press, New York, New York.
Library of Congress Catalog Card Number: 84-82204

Golden®, Golden Press®, and Griffin Design are trademarks of
Western Publishing Company, Inc.

ISBN 0-307-09444-8

Contents

Foreword

Those honest-to-goodness words "home cooking" really ring true when you stop thinking about delicious homemade soups and stews—and actually start making them. With a happy marriage of flavors and textures, you can create a just-right starter, a build-around light meal or a hearty all-out main event. That's what this cookbook is all about. With these recipes, you can turn out one super soup or stew after another.

If there's time, start with homemade broth for the perfect Madrilene, or take a short cut and serve a ready-in-minutes tomato-yogurt soup. For heartier fare, choose a wholesome Beef and Barley Soup or a classic Black Bean Soup. And remember the always-welcome gumbos and chowders for the heartiest of appetites!

You'll find all your family's favorites here, from Cream of Tomato Soup to Oyster Stew. But you'll find some other families' favorites, too. Couscous has been a North African tradition for centuries, Bouillabaise is "down-home cooking" to the French and Gazpacho is a cold soup-salad favorite of the Spanish. No matter how or when you serve them, these soups and stews are all world-class winners.

And, of course, all of the recipes have been thoroughly tested in the Betty Crocker Kitchens—your guarantee of blue-ribbon mealtimes for everyday and special occasions.

Betty Crocker

Soup Beginnings

*Rich homemade broths—for many a good cook,
the heart of a favorite soup and stew.*

*Our three basics—beef, chicken and fish—are used in a
number of recipes throughout this book. Beef and chicken
broth offer a special bonus: The cooked meat can be used
in many other dishes, such as salads, main dishes and
sandwich fillings. Remember, too, that these broths
can be refrigerated or frozen for the future.*

Beef Broth and Cooked Beef

4 **pounds beef shank cross cuts**
12 **cups cold water**
2 **carrots, chopped (about 1 cup)**
2 **stalks celery with leaves, chopped (about 1 cup)**
1 **medium onion, chopped (about ½ cup)**
2 **teaspoons salt**
¼ **teaspoon dried thyme leaves**
10 **peppercorns**
5 **whole cloves**
3 **sprigs parsley**
1 **bay leaf**

Remove beef from bones; cut beef into 1-inch cubes. Remove marrow from center of bones. Heat marrow in Dutch oven over low heat until melted, or heat ¼ cup vegetable oil until hot. Cook and stir beef in marrow until beef is brown. Add water and bones. Heat to boiling; skim foam. Stir in remaining ingredients. Heat to boiling; skim foam. Cover and simmer 3 hours.

Strain broth through cheesecloth-lined sieve. Discard bones, vegetables and seasonings. Skim fat from broth. Clarify broth if desired (see below). Use immediately, or cover and refrigerate broth and beef in separate containers up to 24 hours, or freeze for future use.

10 cups broth and 3½ cups cubed cooked beef.

To clarify broth: Beat 1 egg white, 1 tablespoon water and 1 broken egg shell. Stir into strained broth. Heat to boiling, stirring constantly. Boil 2 minutes. Remove from heat; let stand 5 minutes. Strain through double-thickness cheesecloth.

Note: Hot clarified Beef Broth can be served as an appetizer. Garnish each ½-cup serving with 1 thin lemon slice or 3 thinly sliced mushrooms.

Pictured at right from top: Chicken-Broccoli Chowder (page 62), Crabmeat-Vegetable Soup (page 54) and Shredded Cabbage Soup (page 13)—all prepared with homemade broth.

Chicken Broth and Cooked Chicken

3- to 3½-pound broiler-fryer
  chicken, cut up*
4½ cups cold water
1½ teaspoons salt
½ teaspoon pepper
1 stalk celery with leaves, chopped
  (about ½ cup)
1 medium carrot, sliced (about
  ½ cup)
1 small onion, sliced
1 sprig parsley

Remove any excess fat from chicken. Place chicken, giblets (except liver) and neck in Dutch oven. Add remaining ingredients. Heat to boiling; skim foam. Reduce heat; cover and simmer until thickest pieces of chicken are done, about 45 minutes.

Remove chicken from broth; cool chicken just until cool enough to handle, about 10 minutes. Strain broth through cheesecloth-lined sieve. Remove chicken from bones and skin in pieces as large as possible; cut up chicken. Skim fat from broth. Use immediately, or cover and refrigerate broth and chicken in separate containers up to 24 hours, or freeze for future use.

3 to 3½ cups broth and 3 to 4 cups cut-up cooked chicken.

*3 to 3½ pounds chicken necks, backs and giblets can be used to make broth.

Note: To cook 4- to 6-pound stewing chicken, increase water to 7 cups and salt to 1 tablespoon. Increase simmering time to about 2½ hours.

5 to 6 cups broth and about 5 cups cut-up cooked chicken.

Fish Broth

1½ pounds fish bones and trimmings
4 cups cold water
1½ cups dry white wine
1 tablespoon lemon juice
1 teaspoon salt
½ teaspoon ground thyme
1 large celery stalk, chopped
  (about ½ cup)
1 small onion, sliced
3 mushrooms, chopped
3 sprigs parsley
1 bay leaf

Rinse fish bones and trimmings under running cold water; drain. Mix bones, trimmings, and remaining ingredients in Dutch oven. Heat to boiling; skim foam. Reduce heat; cover and simmer 30 minutes. Strain through cheesecloth-lined sieve. Discard skin, bones, vegetables and seasonings. Use immediately, or cover and refrigerate up to 24 hours, or freeze for future use.

5½ cups broth.

Starter Soups

*These tasty, versatile soups will get your meals off to a smart start,
or be the featured fare for a light lunch or supper menu.
There's a generous variety of every kind of light soup,
from delicate clear Oriental specialties to luscious
cream soups and purees. And for a change,
why not do an about-face and serve
a chilly fruit soup for dessert?*

Beef Consommé

2 cans (10½ ounces each)
  condensed beef broth
1⅓ cups water
¼ cup sliced onion
¼ cup sliced carrot
¼ cup sliced celery
⅛ teaspoon dried thyme leaves
2 sprigs parsley
1 small bay leaf

Heat all ingredients to boiling. Reduce heat; cover and simmer 30 minutes. Strain.

8 servings (about ½ cup each).

Ruby Consommé

Heat 1 cup water, 1 cup tomato juice and 2 cans (10½ ounces each) condensed beef consommé until hot. Serve hot or cover and refrigerate until chilled, about 2 hours, and serve over ice cubes. Garnish each serving with cucumber or radish slices if desired.

8 servings (about ½ cup each).

Hot Bouillon

9 cups Beef Broth (page 6)
1 cup sherry, if desired
¼ teaspoon salt
¼ teaspoon onion salt
¼ teaspoon celery salt
¼ teaspoon pepper
¼ teaspoon dried basil leaves

Heat all ingredients until hot.

12 servings (about ¾ cup each).

Sherried Vegetable Bouillon

½ cup sherry
1 can (46 ounces) cocktail vegetable
  juice
1 can (10½ ounces) condensed beef
  broth
  Snipped parsley

Heat all ingredients except parsley until hot. Sprinkle with parsley.

10 servings (about ¾ cup each).

Spicy Bouillon

5 cups water
2 tablespoons instant beef or
    chicken bouillon
1 tablespoon lemon juice
½ teaspoon Worcestershire sauce
½ teaspoon prepared horseradish

Heat all ingredients to boiling. Boil uncovered, stirring occasionally, 5 minutes.

10 servings (about ½ cup each).

Jellied Madrilene

2 envelopes unflavored gelatin
1 can (18 ounces) tomato juice
3 chicken bouillon cubes
2 cups boiling water
½ teaspoon grated onion
⅛ teaspoon salt
    Dash of pepper
    Lemon wedges

Sprinkle gelatin on tomato juice to soften. Dissolve bouillon cubes in boiling water; add to gelatin mixture, stirring until gelatin is dissolved. Stir in onion, salt and pepper. Refrigerate until set, 4 to 6 hours. To serve, break up with fork; garnish with lemon wedges.

8 servings (about ½ cup each).

Madrilene

2½ cups Beef Broth (page 6)
2½ cups Chicken Broth (page 8)
2½ cups tomato juice
10 thin lemon slices

Heat all ingredients except lemon slices until hot. Garnish each serving with lemon slice.

10 servings (about ¾ cup each).

Quick Borsch

1 can (16 ounces) shoestring beets,
    undrained
1 can (10½ ounces) condensed beef
    broth
1 cup shredded cabbage
2 tablespoons minced onion
1 teaspoon sugar
1 teaspoon lemon juice
    Dairy sour cream

Heat beets, broth, cabbage, onion and sugar to boiling; reduce heat. Simmer uncovered 5 minutes. Stir in lemon juice. (At this point, soup can be served hot if desired.) Cover and refrigerate soup until chilled, no longer than 24 hours. Top each serving with spoonful of sour cream.

7 servings (about ½ cup each).

French Onion Soup

4 medium onions, sliced
2 tablespoons margarine or butter
1½ cups water
⅛ teaspoon pepper
⅛ teaspoon dried thyme leaves
1 bay leaf
2 cans (10½ ounces each)
    condensed beef broth
4 slices French bread, toasted
1 cup shredded Swiss cheese
    (about 4 ounces)
¼ cup grated Parmesan cheese

Cover and cook onions in margarine in 3-quart saucepan over low heat, stirring occasionally, until tender, 20 to 30 minutes. Add water, pepper, thyme, bay leaf and broth. Heat to boiling; reduce heat. Cover and simmer 15 minutes.

Set oven control to broil and/or 550°. Place bread slices on cookie sheet. Broil with tops about 5 inches from heat until golden brown, about 1 minute. Turn; broil until golden brown. Place bread in 4 ovenproof bowls or individual casseroles. Pour in onions and broth; top with Swiss cheese. Sprinkle with Parmesan cheese.

Place bowls in jelly roll pan or on cookie sheet. Broil with tops about 5 inches from heat just until cheese is melted and golden brown, 1 to 2 minutes. Serve with additional French bread if desired.

4 servings.

Shredded Cabbage Soup

2 medium onions, thinly sliced
3 tablespoons bacon fat, margarine
 or butter
5 cups Beef Broth (page 6)
1 small head green cabbage,
 coarsely shredded (about
 5 cups)
2 medium potatoes, cubed (about
 2 cups)
2 carrots, sliced (about 1 cup)
1 stalk celery (with leaves), sliced
 (about ½ cup)
2 tomatoes, cut up (about 2 cups)
1 teaspoon salt
 Freshly ground pepper
 Dairy sour cream
 Snipped dill weed or parsley

Cook and stir onions in bacon fat in Dutch oven until tender. Add Beef Broth, cabbage, potatoes, carrots and celery. Heat to boiling; reduce heat. Cover and simmer until vegetables are tender, about 20 minutes. Stir in tomatoes, salt and pepper. Simmer uncovered about 10 minutes. Top each serving with sour cream; garnish with dill weed. *(Pictured on page 7.)*

12 servings (about ¾ cup each).

Oriental Beef Soup

½ pound beef flank or boneless
 sirloin steak
½ teaspoon cornstarch
½ teaspoon salt
½ teaspoon chopped gingerroot
½ teaspoon vegetable oil
½ teaspoon soy sauce
 Dash of white pepper
3 large stalks bok choy or celery
 cabbage
4 cups Chicken Broth (page 8) or
 Beef Broth (page 6)
1 teaspoon salt

Trim fat from beef; cut beef with grain into 2-inch strips. Cut strips across grain into ⅛-inch slices. Toss beef, cornstarch, ½ teaspoon salt, the gingerroot, vegetable oil, soy sauce and white pepper in glass or plastic bowl. Cover and refrigerate 20 minutes.

Cut bok choy (with leaves) into pieces, 2 x ½ inch. Heat Chicken Broth to boiling in 3-quart saucepan. Add bok choy and 1 teaspoon salt; heat to boiling. Boil uncovered 2 minutes. Stir in beef; heat to boiling. Boil uncovered 1 minute.

12 servings (about ½ cup each).

Wonton Soup

½ **pound ground pork**
1 **green onion (with top), chopped**
2 **teaspoons soy sauce**
½ **teaspoon cornstarch**
¼ **teaspoon ground ginger**
¼ **teaspoon salt**
24 **wonton skins**
5 **cups water**
7½ **cups Chicken Broth (page 8)**
1 **tablespoon soy sauce**
1 **cup spinach (about 1 ounce),**
   torn into small pieces, or 1 cup
   snipped watercress

Cook and stir pork and green onion until pork is brown; drain. Mix pork, green onion, 2 teaspoons soy sauce, the cornstarch, ginger and salt. Place 1 teaspoon filling on center of each wonton skin. Moisten edges with water. Fold each skin in half to form triangle; press edges to seal. Pull bottom corners of triangle down and overlap slightly. Moisten one corner with water; pinch to seal. (Wontons can be covered and refrigerated no longer than 24 hours.)

Heat 5 cups water to boiling in Dutch oven; add wontons. Heat to boiling; reduce heat. Simmer uncovered 2 minutes. (Wontons will break apart if overcooked.) Drain. Heat Chicken Broth and 1 tablespoon soy sauce to boiling in 3-quart saucepan; add spinach. Heat just to boiling. Place 3 wontons and 1 cup hot broth in each soup bowl.

8 servings (about 1 cup broth each).

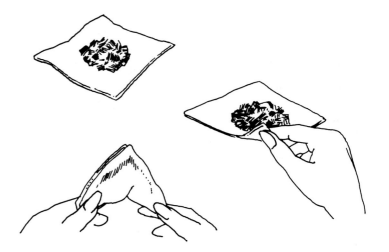

Lemon Soup

1 can (10 ¾ ounces) condensed
   chicken broth
1 cup water
2 tablespoons lemon juice
1 egg
6 thin lemon slices

Beat all ingredients except lemon slices in 1-quart sauce-pan with hand beater until blended. Heat over low heat, stirring constantly, just until hot (do not boil or eggs will curdle). Garnish each serving with lemon slice.

6 servings (about ½ cup each).

Watercress Soup

6 cups Chicken Broth (page 8)
1 teaspoon monosodium
   glutamate, if desired
3 thin slices gingerroot
   Dash of salt
1½ to 2 cups snipped watercress
2 green onions (with tops), thinly
   sliced

Heat Chicken Broth, monosodium glutamate, gingerroot and salt to boiling in 2-quart saucepan. Cook uncovered over high heat 5 minutes. Remove gingerroot from broth; stir in watercress. Cook uncovered over medium heat 15 minutes. Garnish each serving with green onions.

8 servings (about ¾ cup each).

Spinach-Chicken Soup

1 whole chicken breast (about
   1 pound)
½ teaspoon cornstarch
½ teaspoon salt
   Dash of pepper
4 cups Chicken Broth (page 8)
3 thin slices gingerroot
8 ounces spinach, torn into bite-size
   pieces (about 8 cups)
1 teaspoon salt
⅛ teaspoon white pepper

Remove chicken from bones and skin; cut into shreds. Toss chicken, cornstarch, ½ teaspoon salt and dash of pepper. Heat Chicken Broth and gingerroot to boiling in 3-quart saucepan. Stir in chicken; heat to boiling. Stir in spinach, 1 teaspoon salt and the white pepper. Heat to boiling; reduce heat. Cover and simmer until spinach is tender, about 2 minutes. Remove gingerroot.

6 servings (about 1 cup each).

Egg Drop Soup

3 cups Chicken Broth (page 8)
1 teaspoon salt
  Dash of white pepper
1 medium green onion (with top), chopped
2 eggs, slightly beaten

Heat Chicken Broth, salt and white pepper to boiling in 2-quart saucepan. Stir green onion into eggs. Pour egg mixture slowly into broth, stirring constantly with fork, to form shreds of egg.

4 servings (about ¾ cup each).

Garlic Soup

3 cloves garlic, crushed
2 tablespoons vegetable oil
2 slices white bread, cut into small pieces
4 cups Chicken Broth (page 8)
½ teaspoon salt
¼ teaspoon pepper
1 egg, slightly beaten

Cook and stir garlic in oil in 3-quart saucepan until brown; add bread. Cook and stir until light brown. Stir in Chicken Broth, salt and pepper. Heat to boiling; reduce heat. Cover and simmer 20 minutes.

Gradually stir at least half of the hot mixture into egg. Blend into hot mixture in saucepan. Boil and stir 1 minute. Sprinkle with snipped parsley if desired.

8 servings (about ½ cup each).

Clear Japanese Soup

Heat 3 cups Chicken Broth (page 8) and 1 teaspoon soy sauce to boiling, stirring occasionally. Top each serving with 1 to 3 Garnishes (below). *(Pictured at right.)*

4 servings (about ¾ cup each).

Garnishes
Thinly sliced mushrooms, green onion strips, celery leaves, thinly sliced lemon or lime, thinly sliced carrot, strips of lemon peel.

Pictured at right: Clear Japanese Soup

Fresh Fruit Soup

3 tablespoons sugar
3 tablespoons cornstarch
⅛ teaspoon salt
1¼ cups medium red wine
1 cup water
1½ cups cranberry juice cocktail
3 cups fresh fruit, such as
    strawberries, blueberries,
    bananas, seedless green grapes,
    cantaloupe, pitted cherries

Mix sugar, cornstarch and salt in 3-quart saucepan; stir in wine and water. Heat to boiling, stirring constantly. Boil and stir 1 minute. Remove from heat; stir in cranberry juice. Cover loosely and refrigerate until chilled.

Stir in fruit. Top each serving with spoonful of sour cream or whipped cream if desired.

9 servings (about ¾ cup each).

Dried Fruit Soup

1 package (about 12 ounces) mixed
    dried fruit, such as prunes,
    apricots, peaches, pears, raisins
    (2 cups)
½ cup sugar
1½ cups water
1½ cups grape juice or cranberry
    juice cocktail
2 tablespoons quick-cooking
    tapioca
¼ teaspoon salt
2 or 3 thin slices lemon, if desired
3-inch cinnamon stick
1 can (8 ounces) pitted dark sweet
    cherries, undrained

Heat all ingredients except cherries to boiling in 3-quart saucepan, stirring occasionally. Reduce heat; cover and simmer until fruit is tender, 30 to 40 minutes. Stir in cherries and heat. Serve warm or refrigerate until chilled.

8 servings (about ¾ cup each).

Cream of Cherry Soup

1 pound dark sweet cherries, pitted
    and cut into fourths
½ cup sugar
3 cups water
1 teaspoon lemon juice
¼ teaspoon cardamom seed
2 tablespoons cornstarch
2 tablespoons water
½ cup dairy sour cream
⅓ cup dry red wine, chilled
8 whole dark sweet cherries

Heat cut-up cherries, sugar, 3 cups water, the lemon juice and cardamom seed to boiling. Reduce heat; simmer uncovered until cherries are tender, about 10 minutes. Pour half the cherry mixture into blender container. Cover and blend on high speed until smooth. Repeat with remaining mixture. Return to saucepan; heat to boiling. Mix cornstarch and 2 tablespoons water; stir gradually into cherries. Continue boiling, stirring constantly, until soup thickens and becomes clear, about 2 minutes. Cover and refrigerate until chilled, at least 4 hours. Just before serving, stir in sour cream and wine. Garnish each serving with whole cherry.

8 servings (about ½ cup each).

Cold Cucumber Soup

2 medium cucumbers
1½ cups plain yogurt
½ teaspoon salt
¼ teaspoon dried mint flakes
⅛ teaspoon white pepper

Cut 7 thin slices from cucumber; reserve. Cut remaining cucumber into ¾-inch chunks. Place half of the cucumber chunks and ¼ cup of the yogurt in blender container. Cover and blend on high speed until smooth. Add remaining cucumber, the salt, mint and white pepper. Cover and blend until smooth. Add remaining yogurt; cover and blend on low speed until smooth. Cover and refrigerate until chilled, at least 1 hour. Garnish with reserved cucumber slices.

7 servings (about ½ cup each).

Chilled Yogurt-Vegetable Soup

¼ cup margarine or butter
1 cup thinly sliced mushrooms
4 medium carrots, shredded
2 small zucchini, shredded
⅓ cup finely chopped onion
1 teaspoon dried dill weed
4 cups Chicken Broth (page 8)
1 package (10 ounces) frozen green
   peas
2 cups plain yogurt

Heat margarine in 4-quart saucepan over medium heat until melted. Stir in mushrooms, carrots, zucchini, onion and dill weed. Cover and cook 2½ minutes; stir once. Cover and cook until vegetables are crisp-tender, about 2½ minutes longer; add broth and peas. Heat to boiling over high heat; remove from heat. Pour into bowl; cool completely. Stir in yogurt; cover and refrigerate until chilled. Sprinkle with salt and pepper if desired. Refrigerate any remaining soup.

12 servings (about ¾ cup each).

Vichyssoise

1 medium onion, sliced
2 teaspoons margarine or butter
2 medium potatoes, thinly sliced
1 small stalk celery, chopped (about ¼ cup)
¼ teaspoon salt
1 can (10¾ ounces) condensed chicken broth
1 cup half-and-half
¼ teaspoon salt
⅛ teaspoon pepper
½ to ⅔ cup half-and-half

Cook and stir onion in margarine in 3-quart saucepan over medium heat until onion is tender; reduce heat. Stir in potatoes, celery, ¼ teaspoon salt and the broth. Cover and simmer until potatoes are soft, 30 to 40 minutes. Press potato mixture through sieve. Return potato mixture to saucepan. Stir in 1 cup half-and-half, ¼ teaspoon salt and the pepper. Heat over medium heat, stirring constantly, until hot and bubbly. (At this point, soup can be served hot if desired.) Cover and refrigerate soup until chilled, at least 4 hours.

Just before serving, stir ½ to ⅔ cup half-and-half into soup. Garnish with snipped chives and paprika if desired.

6 servings (about ½ cup each) cold, 3 servings (about 1 cup each) hot.

Gazpacho

3 cups tomato juice
2 beef bouillon cubes
2 tomatoes, chopped
½ cup chopped cucumber
¼ cup chopped green pepper
¼ cup chopped onion
¼ cup wine vinegar
2 tablespoons vegetable oil
1 teaspoon salt
1 teaspoon Worcestershire sauce
6 drops red pepper sauce
   Accompaniments (herbed croutons and about ⅔ cup each chopped cucumber, tomato, green pepper and onion)

Heat tomato juice to boiling. Add bouillon cubes; stir until dissolved. Stir in remaining ingredients except Accompaniments. Refrigerate several hours. Serve with Accompaniments.

10 servings (about ½ cup each).

Pictured at right: Gazpacho (top) and Vichyssoise

Cream of Almond Soup

1 tablespoon margarine or butter
1 tablespoon all-purpose flour
½ teaspoon salt
⅛ teaspoon pepper
1 can (10¾ ounces) condensed
    chicken broth
2 cups half-and-half
⅓ cup toasted sliced almonds
    (see Note)
½ teaspoon grated lemon peel

Heat margarine in 1½-quart saucepan over low heat until melted. Stir in flour, salt and pepper. Cook over low heat, stirring constantly, until smooth and bubbly; remove from heat. Stir in broth. Heat to boiling, stirring constantly. Boil and stir 1 minute; reduce heat. Stir in remaining ingredients; heat just until soup is hot (do not boil).

8 servings (about ½ cup each).

Note: To toast almonds, spread almonds in shallow pan. Heat in 325° oven until golden, stirring occasionally.

Avocado Soup

1 can (10¾ ounces) condensed
    chicken broth
1 tablespoon lemon juice
1 teaspoon chopped onion
¾ teaspoon curry powder
    Dash of garlic powder
1 large avocado, pared and cut up
⅔ cup plain yogurt

Heat broth until hot. Place broth and the remaining ingredients except yogurt in blender container. Cover and blend on low speed until smooth, 15 to 30 seconds. Add yogurt. Cover and blend just until mixed. Serve warm.

4 servings (about ½ cup each).

Beer and Cheese Soup

1 medium onion, chopped (about
    ½ cup)
2 tablespoons margarine or butter
½ cup finely chopped carrots
½ cup finely chopped celery
1 bottle or can (12 ounces) beer
2 cups Chicken Broth (page 8)
1 teaspoon salt
1 teaspoon ground cumin
¼ teaspoon ground nutmeg
    Dash of ground cloves
    Dash of pepper
1 cup dairy sour cream
4 ounces Cheddar or Monterey Jack
    cheese, cut into ¼-inch cubes
    (about 1 cup)

Cook and stir onion in margarine in 2-quart saucepan until tender. Stir in carrots, celery and beer. Heat to boiling; reduce heat. Cover and simmer 10 minutes. Stir in Chicken Broth, salt, cumin, nutmeg, cloves and pepper. Heat to boiling; reduce heat. Cover and simmer 30 minutes. Remove from heat; stir in sour cream. Sprinkle with cheese.

7 servings (about ¾ cup each).

Cream of Carrot Soup

1 small onion, chopped (about
   ¼ cup)
2 tablespoons margarine or butter
2 cups chopped carrots (about
   1 pound)
2 tablespoons white wine
3 cups Chicken Broth (page 8)
1 teaspoon salt
⅛ teaspoon ground nutmeg
   Dash of pepper
1 cup whipping cream

Cook and stir onion in margarine in 2-quart saucepan until tender. Add carrots and wine. Heat to boiling; reduce heat. Cover and simmer 10 minutes. Stir in Chicken Broth, salt, nutmeg and pepper. Heat to boiling; reduce heat. Cover and simmer until carrots are tender, 30 minutes.

Pour half the carrot mixture into blender container. Cover and blend on medium speed until smooth; strain. Repeat with remaining mixture. Heat until hot. Beat whipping cream until stiff; stir into soup.

6 servings (about ¾ cup each).

Creamy Cauliflower Soup

2 cups water
1 medium head cauliflower (about
   2 pounds), broken into
   flowerets (about 6 cups)
1 large stalk celery, chopped
   (about ¾ cup)
1 medium onion, chopped (about
   ½ cup)
1 tablespoon lemon juice
2 tablespoons margarine or butter
2 tablespoons all-purpose flour
2½ cups water
1 tablespoon instant chicken
   bouillon
¾ teaspoon salt
⅛ teaspoon pepper
   Dash of ground nutmeg
½ cup whipping cream

Heat 2 cups water to boiling in 3-quart saucepan. Add cauliflower, celery, onion and lemon juice. Cover; heat to boiling. Cook until tender, about 10 minutes; do not drain. Place in blender container. Cover and blend until uniform consistency.

Heat margarine in 3-quart saucepan over low heat until melted. Stir in flour. Cook, stirring constantly, until mixture is smooth and bubbly.

Remove from heat; stir in 2½ cups water. Heat to boiling, stirring constantly. Boil and stir 1 minute. Stir in cauliflower mixture, bouillon (dry), salt, pepper and nutmeg. Heat just to boiling. Stir in cream; heat just until hot (do not boil). Serve with grated cheese if desired.

8 servings (about 1 cup each).

Cream of Celery Soup

Celery (right)
1 teaspoon finely chopped onion
2 tablespoons margarine or butter
3 tablespoons all-purpose flour
1 teaspoon salt
⅛ teaspoon pepper
2 cups Chicken Broth (page 8)
2 cups milk

Cook Celery. Cook and stir onion in margarine over low heat until tender. Stir in flour, salt and pepper. Cook over low heat, stirring constantly, until mixture is bubbly. Remove from heat; stir in Chicken Broth and milk. Heat to boiling, stirring constantly. Boil and stir 1 minute. Stir in Celery; heat until hot.

6 servings (about ¾ cup each).

Celery

Heat 1 inch salted water (½ teaspoon salt to 1 cup water) to boiling. Add 1 cup diced celery. Cover and heat to boiling. Cook until tender, 15 to 20 minutes; drain.

Cream of Mushroom Soup

8 ounces mushrooms
4 tablespoons margarine or butter
1 medium onion, chopped (about ½ cup)
¼ cup all-purpose flour
1 teaspoon salt
¼ teaspoon white pepper
1¼ cups water
1 can (10¾ ounces) condensed chicken broth
1 cup half-and-half
Snipped parsley

Slice enough mushrooms to measure 1 cup; chop remaining mushrooms. Cook and stir sliced mushrooms in 2 tablespoons of the margarine in 3-quart saucepan over low heat until golden brown. Remove mushrooms with slotted spoon.

Cook and stir chopped mushrooms and onion in remaining margarine until onion is tender. Stir in flour, salt and white pepper. Cook over low heat, stirring constantly, about 1 minute. Remove from heat; stir in water and broth. Heat to boiling, stirring constantly. Boil and stir 1 minute. Stir in half-and-half and sliced mushrooms; heat just until hot (do not boil). Garnish each serving with parsley.

6 servings (about ¾ cup each).

Quick Creamy Potato Soup

3½ cups milk
2 tablespoons margarine or butter
2 tablespoons finely chopped onion or 1 tablespoon instant minced onion
1½ teaspoons salt
¼ teaspoon celery salt
⅛ teaspoon pepper
1⅓ cups mashed potato mix
Paprika
Snipped parsley

Heat milk, margarine, onion, salt, celery salt and pepper to scalding in 2-quart saucepan. Stir in mashed potato mix; continue cooking, stirring constantly, until smooth. (Soup should be consistency of whipping cream.) Garnish each serving with paprika and parsley.

8 servings (about ½ cup each).

Chunky Potato Soup

6 slices bacon, cut up
1 large onion, chopped (about 1 cup)
2 medium stalks celery, chopped (about 1 cup)
1 can (16 ounces) whole potatoes, drained and coarsely chopped
1 can (10¾ ounces) condensed chicken broth
½ cup water
¼ teaspoon dried thyme leaves
⅛ teaspoon pepper
1 cup milk

Fry bacon in 3-quart saucepan until crisp. Remove bacon; drain and reserve. Pour off all but 2 tablespoons bacon fat. Cook and stir onion and celery in bacon fat until celery is tender, about 6 minutes. Stir in potatoes, broth, water, thyme, and pepper. Heat to boiling; reduce heat. Cover and simmer 10 minutes. Stir in milk and bacon; heat just until hot (do not boil).

8 servings (about ½ cup each).

Summer Vegetable Soup

2 cups water
1 cup cut fresh or frozen green beans
¾ cup fresh or frozen green peas
¼ small cauliflower, separated into flowerets
2 small carrots, sliced
1 medium potato, cubed
2 ounces spinach, cut up (about 2 cups)
2 cups milk
2 tablespoons all-purpose flour
¼ cup whipping cream
1½ teaspoons salt
⅛ teaspoon pepper
Snipped dill weed or parsley

Heat water, beans, peas, cauliflower, carrots and potato to boiling in 3-quart saucepan; reduce heat. Cover and simmer until vegetables are crisp-tender, 10 to 15 minutes.

Add spinach; cook uncovered about 1 minute. Mix ¼ cup of the milk and the flour; gradually stir into vegetable mixture. Boil and stir 1 minute. Stir in remaining milk, the cream, salt and pepper. Heat just until hot (do not boil). Garnish each serving with dill weed.

10 servings (¾ cup each).

Spinach-Asparagus Soup

5 cups Chicken Broth (page 8)
¼ cup uncooked regular rice
½ teaspoon salt
8 ounces asparagus, cut into 1-inch
   pieces or 1 package (10 ounces)
   frozen cut asparagus
1 medium carrot, thinly sliced
   (about ½ cup)
12 ounces spinach, shredded or finely
   chopped
4 Frozen Cream Soup Flavor
   Chunks (right)

Heat Chicken Broth, rice and salt to boiling in 3-quart saucepan, stirring once or twice; reduce heat. Cover and simmer 5 minutes. Stir in asparagus and carrot. Add spinach and Frozen Cream Soup Flavor Chunks, stirring until flavor chunks are melted and soup is thickened, about 5 minutes.

8 servings (about ¾ cup each).

Frozen Cream Soup Flavor Chunks

1 cup all-purpose flour
1 cup instant nonfat dry milk
1 cup margarine or butter, softened
2 tablespoons parsley flakes
1 tablespoon onion powder
½ teaspoon white pepper

Mix all ingredients until dough leaves side of bowl and rounds into a ball. Drop mixture by rounded tablespoonfuls onto waxed paper. Freeze until firm, about 1 hour. Freeze in covered container or plastic bag.

12 soup flavor chunks.

Drop the dough for the soup flavor chunks by rounded tablespoonfuls onto waxed paper. Freeze about 1 hour.

Cream of Tomato Soup

1 can (16 ounces) whole tomatoes,
    undrained
1 small onion, sliced
¼ teaspoon celery salt
¼ teaspoon ground cinnamon
⅛ teaspoon ground cloves
3 tablespoons margarine or butter
3 tablespoons all-purpose flour
¾ teaspoon salt
3 cups milk

Cook tomatoes, onion, celery salt, cinnamon and cloves 15 minutes. Place in blender container. Cover and blend until uniform consistency. Heat margarine in 1½-quart saucepan over low heat until melted. Stir in flour and salt. Cook over low heat, stirring constantly, until mixture is smooth and bubbly. Remove from heat; stir in milk. Heat to boiling, stirring constantly. Boil and stir 1 minute. Stir in tomato mixture. Heat just to boiling.

7 servings (about ¾ cup each).

Quick Tomato-Yogurt Soup

Mix 1 can (10¾ ounces) condensed tomato soup and ⅔ cup plain yogurt in 1-quart saucepan. Heat over medium heat, stirring constantly, until hot.

4 servings (about ½ cup each).

Cream of Vegetable Soup

3 cups water
¼ cup uncooked spiral macaroni
1 package (10 ounces) frozen peas
    and carrots or mixed vegetables
1 cup shredded Cheddar cheese
    (about 4 ounces)
½ teaspoon salt
½ teaspoon dry mustard
2 Frozen Cream Soup Flavor
    Chunks (opposite page)

Heat water to boiling in 2-quart saucepan. Stir in macaroni and peas and carrots. Heat to boiling; reduce heat. Cover and simmer until vegetables are tender, about 5 minutes. Add cheese, salt, mustard and Frozen Cream Soup Flavor Chunks, stirring until flavor chunks are melted and soup is thickened, about 5 minutes.

8 servings (about ½ cup each).

Zucchini Soup

1 small onion, chopped (about ¼ cup)
1 tablespoon margarine or butter
2 cups Chicken Broth (page 8)
2 tablespoons finely chopped canned roasted green chilies
½ teaspoon salt
⅛ teaspoon pepper
2 small zucchini, chopped
1 can (8¾ ounces) whole kernel corn, drained*
1 cup milk
2 ounces Monterey Jack cheese, cut into ¼-inch cubes (about ½ cup)
Ground nutmeg
Snipped parsley

Cook and stir onion in margarine in 2-quart saucepan until tender. Stir in Chicken Broth, chilies, salt, pepper, zucchini and corn. Heat to boiling; reduce heat. Cover and cook until zucchini is tender, about 5 minutes. Stir in milk; heat just until hot (do not boil). Add cheese; garnish with nutmeg and parsley.

7 servings (about ¾ cup each).

*1 package (10 ounces) frozen whole kernel corn can be substituted for the canned corn.

Broccoli-Chicken Soup

1 cup water
1 tablespoon lemon juice
12 ounces broccoli, cut up
1 medium stalk celery, chopped (about ½ cup)
1 small onion, chopped (about ¼ cup)
1 tablespoon margarine or butter
1 tablespoon all-purpose flour
1¼ cups water
1½ teaspoon instant chicken bouillon
1 teaspoon salt
Dash of ground nutmeg
1½ cups cut-up cooked chicken (page 8)
¾ cup half-and-half

Heat 1 cup water and the lemon juice to boiling in 3-quart saucepan. Add broccoli, celery and onion. Cover and heat to boiling; reduce heat. Simmer until vegetables are tender, about 15 minutes; do not drain. Place in blender container. Cover and blend on medium speed, stopping blender frequently to scrape sides, until mixture is of uniform consistency, about 45 seconds.

Heat margarine in 3-quart saucepan over low heat until melted. Stir in flour. Cook, stirring constantly, until mixture is smooth and bubbly; remove from heat. Stir in 1¼ cups water. Heat to boiling, stirring constantly. Boil and stir 1 minute. Stir in broccoli mixture, bouillion (dry), salt and nutmeg. Heat just to boiling. Stir in chicken and half-and-half. Heat just until hot (do not boil). Garnish each serving with yogurt, sour cream or lemon slice if desired.

8 servings (about ½ cup each).

Wild Rice-Chicken Soup

⅓ cup uncooked wild rice
4 cups Chicken Broth (page 8)
½ cup sliced mushrooms
¼ cup chopped celery
1 small onion, chopped (about ¼ cup)
1 clove garlic, crushed
½ teaspoon salt
¼ teaspoon pepper
¼ cup margarine or butter
⅓ cup all-purpose flour
1 cup cut-up cooked chicken (page 8)
1 cup whipping cream
2 tablespoons dry white wine

Wash wild rice by placing in wire strainer; run cold water through it, lifting rice with fingers to clean thoroughly. Heat rice and Chicken Broth to boiling, stirring once or twice; reduce heat. Cover and simmer until tender, 40 to 50 minutes.

Cook and stir mushrooms, celery, onion, garlic, salt and pepper in margarine in 3-quart saucepan until celery is tender, about 6 minutes. Stir in flour. Cook over low heat, stirring constantly, until mixture is bubbly; remove from heat. Stir in cut-up chicken and Chicken Broth with rice. Heat to boiling, stirring constantly. Stir in cream and wine; heat just until hot (do not boil).

10 servings (about ½ cup each).

Tomato-Seafood Cream Soup

2 tablespoons finely chopped onion
¼ cup margarine or butter
¼ cup all-purpose flour
¼ teaspoon salt
⅛ teaspoon pepper
2 cups tomato juice
1 cup whipping cream
1 cup milk
1½ teaspoons Worcestershire sauce
¼ teaspoon monosodium glutamate, if desired
4 drops red pepper sauce
1 can (5 ounces) lobster, drained and broken apart, or 1 can (4¼ ounces) tiny shrimp, rinsed and drained
3 tablespoons sherry flavoring
½ cup chilled whipping cream

Cook and stir onion in margarine in 3-quart saucepan until tender. Stir in flour, salt and pepper. Cook, stirring constantly, until smooth and bubbly. Remove from heat; gradually stir in tomato juice, 1 cup cream, the milk, Worcestershire sauce, monosodium glutamate and red pepper sauce. Heat to boiling, stirring constantly. Boil 1 minute. Reserve few pieces lobster. Stir remaining lobster and sherry flavoring into soup. Heat just until hot (do not boil). Beat whipping cream in chilled bowl until stiff. Garnish each serving with reserved lobster pieces and whipped cream.

6 servings (about ¾ cup each).

Shrimp Bisque

1 teaspoon grated onion
1 tablespoon margarine or butter
1 tablespoon all-purpose flour
2 teaspoons snipped parsley
1 teaspoon salt
⅛ teaspoon celery salt
⅛ teaspoon pepper
2 cups milk
1 cup Chicken Broth (page 8) or water
1 can (7 ounces) shrimp, drained and chopped (reserve liquid)

Cook and stir onion in margarine over low heat. Stir in flour, parsley, salt, celery salt and pepper. Cook, stirring constantly, until mixture is smooth and bubbly. Remove from heat; stir in milk and Chicken Broth. Heat to boiling, stirring constantly. Boil and stir 1 minute. Stir in shrimp and liquid.

8 servings (about ½ cup each).

Shrimp Soup

½ pound small fresh or frozen raw shrimp
4 cups Chicken Broth (page 8)
¼ cup tomato and yellow chili sauce
½ teapoon salt
⅛ teaspoon ground saffron
Dash of pepper
1 teaspoon cornstarch
1 tablespoon cold water
½ cup half-and-half
¼ cup snipped parsley

Peel shrimp. (If shrimp is frozen, do not thaw; peel under running cold water.) Make a shallow cut lengthwise down back of each shrimp; wash out sand vein. Chop shrimp. Place shrimp, 1 cup of the Chicken Broth and the chili sauce in blender container. Cover and blend on high speed until smooth. Heat shrimp mixture, the remaining broth, salt, saffron and pepper to boiling.

Mix cornstarch and water; stir into shrimp mixture. Heat to boiling; cook and stir 1 minute. Remove from heat; stir in half-and-half. Sprinkle with parsley.

10 servings (about ½ cup each).

Oyster and Green Pea Soup

1 package (10 ounces) frozen green peas
1 tablespoon margarine or butter
1 tablespoon all-purpose flour
1 cup milk
1 cup fresh oysters, pureed or minced
1 teaspoon salt
⅛ teaspoon pepper
½ cup whipping cream

Cook peas as directed on package. Drain; place in blender container. Cover and blend until uniform consistency. Heat margarine in saucepan until melted. Stir in flour. Cook, stirring constantly, until mixture is smooth and bubbly. Remove from heat; stir in peas, milk, oysters, salt and pepper. Heat to boiling, stirring constantly. Boil and stir 1 minute. Stir in cream; heat just until hot (do not boil).

6 servings (about ½ cup each).

Hearty Soups

*With any of these wholesome and delicious soups you can create
the kind of main course that makes everyone feel cared for.
Easy on the cook, too: Just serve with a crisp
tossed salad and an interesting bread.*

Chunky Beef-Noodle Soup

1 pound beef boneless round
    steak, cut into ¾-inch pieces
1 large onion, chopped (about
    1 cup)
2 cloves garlic, finely chopped
1 tablespoon vegetable oil
2 cups water
2 teaspoons chili powder
1½ teaspoons salt
½ teaspoon dried oregano leaves
1 can (16 ounces) whole tomatoes,
    undrained
1 can (10½ ounces) condensed beef
    broth
2 ounces uncooked egg noodles
    (about 1 cup)
1 medium green pepper, coarsely
    chopped (about 1 cup)
¼ cup snipped parsley

Cook and stir beef, onion and garlic in oil in Dutch oven until beef is brown, about 15 minutes. Stir in water, chili powder, salt, oregano, tomatoes and broth; break up tomatoes with fork. Heat to boiling; reduce heat. Cover and simmer until beef is tender, 1½ to 2 hours.

Skim excess fat from soup. Stir noodles and green pepper into soup. Heat to boiling; reduce heat. Simmer uncovered until noodles are tender, about 10 minutes. Stir in parsley.

4 servings (about 1½ cups each).

Beef and Barley Soup

5 slices bacon
1-pound beef chuck roast or steak,
    cut into 1-inch pieces
2 large onions, chopped (about
    2 cups)
2 cloves garlic, finely chopped
2 cups water
¼ cup regular barley
1½ teaspoons paprika
1 teaspoon salt
¼ teaspoon caraway seed
⅛ teaspoon dried marjoram leaves
2 cans (10½ ounces each)
    condensed beef broth
3 medium potatoes, cut into
    ½-inch pieces (about 3 cups)
2 medium carrots, sliced (about
    1 cup)
2 medium stalks celery, sliced
    (about 1 cup)
1 can (16 ounces) stewed tomatoes
1 package (10 ounces) frozen green
    peas, broken apart
1 can (4 ounces) mushroom stems
    and pieces, undrained

Fry bacon in Dutch oven over medium heat until crisp. Remove bacon; drain and reserve. Cook and stir beef, onions and garlic in bacon fat in Dutch oven until beef is brown. Stir in water, barley, paprika, salt, caraway seed, marjoram and broth. Heat to boiling; reduce heat. Cover and simmer 1½ hours.

Stir in potatoes, carrots, celery, tomatoes, peas and mushrooms. Heat to boiling; reduce heat. Cover and simmer until vegetables are tender, 30 to 40 minutes. Crumble bacon; sprinkle over soup.

5 servings (about 1½ cups each).

Beef and Squash Soup

1½ pounds beef boneless chuck, tip
    or round, cut into ¾-inch
    pieces
2 cups water
2 teaspoons salt
¼ teaspoon ground ginger
⅛ to ¼ teaspoon cayenne pepper
1½ pounds Hubbard squash, pared
    and cut into 1-inch cubes*
2 medium tomatoes, chopped
    (about 2 cups)
1 package (10 ounces) frozen baby
    lima beans

Heat beef, water, salt, ginger and cayenne pepper to boiling in Dutch oven; reduce heat. Cover and simmer 1½ hours. Add squash; cover and cook until beef and squash are tender, 30 to 45 minutes.

Remove squash; place in blender container. Cover and blend until smooth. Return squash to Dutch oven. Add tomatoes and beans. Heat to boiling; reduce heat. Cover and simmer until beans are tender, about 15 minutes. Top each serving with hot cooked rice if desired.

6 servings (about 1 cup each).

*1 package (12 ounces) frozen cooked squash, thawed, can be substituted for the fresh squash; add with tomatoes.

Beef-Vegetable Soup

1 pound beef boneless chuck, tip
    or round, cut into cubes
1 tablespoon vegetable oil
1 cup water
2 teaspoons instant beef bouillon
1½ teaspoons salt
¼ teaspoon dried marjoram leaves
¼ teaspoon dried thyme leaves
¼ teaspoon monosodium
    glutamate, if desired
⅛ teaspoon pepper
1 bay leaf
4 cups water
3 medium carrots, sliced (about
    1½ cups)
1 large stalk celery, sliced (about
    ½ cup)
1 medium onion, chopped (about
    ½ cup)
1 can (16 ounces) whole tomatoes,
    undrained

Cook and stir beef in oil in Dutch oven over medium heat until brown. Stir in 1 cup water, the bouillon (dry), salt, marjoram, thyme, monosodium glutamate, pepper and bay leaf. Cover and simmer until beef is tender, 1 to 1½ hours.

Stir in 4 cups water, the carrots, celery, onion and tomatoes; break up tomatoes with fork. Heat to boiling; reduce heat. Cover and simmer until carrots are tender, about 35 minutes. Remove bay leaf.

6 servings (about 1½ cups each).

Beef-Pasta Vegetable Soup: Cover and simmer until carrots are crisp-tender, about 30 minutes. Stir in ½ cup uncooked macaroni rings. Cover and simmer until macaroni is tender, 7 to 10 minutes.

Borsch

6 cups water
4 ounces dried navy beans (about ½ cup)
1 pound beef boneless chuck, tip or round, cut into cubes
1 smoked pork hock
2½ teaspoons salt
¼ teaspoon pepper
1 can (10½ ounces) condensed beef broth
6 medium beets
6 cups water
1 tablespoon vinegar
1 teaspoon salt
3 cups shredded cabbage
2 medium potatoes, cut into cubes (about 2 cups)
2 medium onions, sliced
2 cloves garlic, chopped
Bouquet garni*
¼ cup red wine vinegar
1 cup dairy sour cream

Heat 6 cups water and the beans to boiling in Dutch oven; boil 2 minutes. Remove from heat; cover and let stand 1 hour.

Add beef, pork, 2½ teaspoons salt, the pepper and broth to beans. Heat to boiling; reduce heat. Cover and simmer until beef is tender, 1 to 1½ hours.

Cut off all but 2 inches of beet tops. Wash beets and leave whole, with root ends attached. Heat 6 cups water, the vinegar and 1 teaspoon salt to boiling. Add beets. Cover and heat to boiling. Cook until tender, 35 to 45 minutes; drain. Run cold water over beets; slip off skins and remove root ends. Shred beets or cut into ¼-inch strips.

Remove pork from Dutch oven; cool slightly. Remove pork from bone; cut into bite-size pieces. Add pork, beets, cabbage, potatoes, onions, garlic and bouquet garni. Cover and simmer 2 hours.

Stir in vinegar; simmer 10 minutes. Remove bouquet garni. Serve with sour cream; sprinkle with snipped dill if desired.

6 servings (about 1½ cups each).

*Tie 2 teaspoons dill seed or 1 sprig dill and 1 tablespoon pickling spice in cheesecloth bag or place in tea ball.

Hamburger Minestrone

2 pounds ground beef
1 large onion, chopped (about 1 cup)
1 clove garlic, finely chopped
2 cups Beef Broth (page 6)
½ cup red wine or water
1 cup uncooked elbow macaroni or broken spaghetti
2 cups shredded cabbage
2 small zucchini, sliced (about 2 cups)
2 stalks celery, sliced (about 1 cup)
1½ teaspoons salt
1½ teaspoons Italian seasoning
1 can (28 ounces) whole tomatoes, undrained
1 can (15 ounces) kidney beans, undrained
1 can (12 ounces) vacuum pack whole kernel corn, undrained
Grated Parmesan cheese

Cook and stir ground beef, onion and garlic in Dutch oven until beef is brown; drain. Stir in remaining ingredients except cheese; break up tomatoes with fork. Heat to boiling; reduce heat. Cover and simmer, stirring occasionally, until macaroni and vegetables are tender, about 30 minutes. Serve with cheese.

10 servings (about 1½ cups each).

Hamburger-Vegetable Soup

1 pound ground beef
2 medium stalks celery, sliced (about 1 cup)
1 tablespoon instant beef bouillon
2 teaspoons parsley flakes
1 teaspoon salt
½ teaspoon nutmeg
1 large onion, chopped (about 1 cup)
1 can (16 ounces) whole tomatoes, undrained
1 can (16 ounces) diced beets, undrained
1 can (16 ounces) diced carrots, drained
2 cups shredded cabbage
1 can (12 ounces) beer

Cook and stir ground beef and celery in Dutch oven until beef is brown; drain. Stir in bouillon (dry), parsley, salt, nutmeg, onion, tomatoes, beets and carrots. Heat to boiling; reduce heat. Cover and simmer 10 minutes. Stir in cabbage and beer. Heat to boiling; reduce heat. Cover and simmer until cabbage is crisp-tender, about 5 minutes.

5 servings (about 1½ cups each).

Beefy Mexican Soup

1 pound ground beef
¼ cup chopped green pepper
1 medium onion, chopped (about ½ cup)
5 cups water
1 teaspoon chili powder
½ teaspoon garlic salt
¼ teaspoon salt
1 can (16 ounces) whole tomatoes, undrained
1 package (7.25 ounces) main dish mix for chili tomato
1 can (8 ounces) whole kernel corn, undrained
2 tablespoons sliced pitted ripe olives

Cook and stir ground beef, green pepper and onion in Dutch oven until beef is brown; drain. Stir in water, chili powder, garlic salt, salt, tomatoes and Sauce Mix; break up tomatoes with fork. Heat to boiling, stirring constantly; reduce heat. Cover and simmer, stirring occasionally, 10 minutes. Stir in Macaroni, corn and olives. Cover and cook 10 minutes longer. Garnish with corn chips if desired.

6 servings (about 1½ cups each).

Pork and Hominy Soup

¼ cup vegetable oil
1 clove garlic
½ pound pork boneless shoulder, cut into cubes
¼ cup all-purpose flour
1 medium onion, chopped (about ½ cup)
¼ cup chopped carrot
¼ cup chopped celery
¼ cup chopped green chilies
1 tablespoon chili powder
1 can (30 ounces) hominy, drained
1 can (15 ounces) pinto beans, drained
3 cups Chicken Broth (page 8)
1 teaspoon salt
¼ teaspoon pepper
1½ teaspoons dried oregano leaves
1 small onion, chopped (about ¼ cup)
¼ cup snipped cilantro

Heat oil and garlic in 3-quart saucepan until hot. Coat pork with flour. Cook and stir pork in oil over medium heat until brown; remove from saucepan. Cook and stir ½ cup onion in same saucepan until tender. Stir in carrot, celery, green chilies, chili powder, hominy and pinto beans. Heat to boiling; reduce heat. Cover and simmer 10 minutes.

Stir pork, Chicken Broth, salt and pepper into vegetable mixture. Heat to boiling; reduce heat. Cover and simmer 30 minutes. Sprinkle with oregano, ¼ cup onion and the cilantro.

4 servings (about 1½ cups each).

Green Bean and Ham Soup

2 cups water
¼ cup uncooked instant rice
1 teaspoon parsley flakes
¼ teaspoon dried savory leaves
1 small onion, thinly sliced
1 can (10 ¾ ounces) condensed
   chicken broth
1 package (10 ounces) frozen cut
   green beans
1 can (8 ounces) sliced carrots,
   undrained
1 can (6¾ ounces) chunk ham

Heat water, rice, parsley, savory, onion, broth and beans to boiling in 2-quart saucepan, stirring occasionally; reduce heat. Cover and simmer until beans are tender, about 5 minutes. Stir in carrots and ham; heat just until hot.

4 servings (about 1¼ cups each).

Creole-style Sausage-Potato Soup

1½ pounds large smoked sausage
   links, cut into 3- to 4-inch
   pieces
2 tablespoons sugar
1 teaspoon salt
2 medium carrots, thinly sliced
   (about 1 cup)
2 medium stalks celery, sliced
   (about 1 cup)
1 envelope (about 1½ ounces)
   onion soup mix
6 cups boiling water
1 can (28 ounces) whole tomatoes,
   undrained
¼ teaspoon oregano
¼ teaspoon red pepper sauce
1 package (5.5 ounces) hash brown
   potato mix with onions
1 package (10 ounces) frozen sliced
   okra, thawed

Place sausage, sugar, salt, carrots, celery and onion soup mix in Dutch oven; add boiling water. Cover and simmer 10 minutes. Add tomatoes; break up with fork. Stir in oregano, pepper sauce, potatoes and okra. Heat to boiling; reduce heat. Cover and simmer until vegetables are tender, 30 to 40 minutes.

8 servings (about 1½ cups each).

Sausage-Vegetable Soup

1 medium onion, chopped (about ½ cup)
2 tablespoons vegetable oil
4 cups water
2 teaspoons salt
½ teaspoon dried chervil leaves
½ teaspoon dried thyme leaves
3 medium carrots, thinly sliced (about 1½ cups)
2 medium stalks celery with leaves, thinly sliced (about 1 cup)
2 medium zucchini, cut lengthwise into halves, then into ¼-inch slices (about 4 cups)
1 pint cherry tomatoes, cut into halves
1 pound kielbasa or Polish sausage, cut into ¼-inch slices
1 can (15 ounces) great northern beans, undrained

Cook and stir onion in oil in Dutch oven until tender. Stir in water, salt, chervil, thyme, carrots and celery. Heat to boiling; reduce heat. Cover and simmer until vegetables are tender, about 30 minutes.

Stir zucchini, tomatoes, sausage and beans into vegetables in Dutch oven. Heat to boiling; reduce heat. Cover and simmer 30 minutes. Skim fat.

5 servings (about 1½ cups each).

Scotch Broth

5 cups water
½ cup regular barley
½ cup dried yellow peas
1 to 2 pounds lamb boneless
   shoulder
5 cups water
5 teaspoons salt
2 medium carrots, chopped (about
   1 cup)
1 turnip, diced
1 small head cabbage, cut up
2 small onions, chopped
¾ cup snipped parsley
2 tablespoons margarine or butter
⅛ teaspoon pepper
1 carrot, grated

Heat 5 cups water, the barley and peas to boiling in Dutch oven; boil 2 minutes. Remove from heat; cover and let stand 1 hour. Heat lamb, 5 cups water and the salt to boiling; reduce heat. Cover and simmer 1 hour. Skim fat. Add to barley mixture with liquid, chopped carrots, turnip, cabbage and onions. Heat to boiling; reduce heat. Cover and simmer until peas are tender, about 1 hour. Stir in remaining ingredients. Cover and simmer 15 minutes.

8 servings (about 1½ cups each).

Economy Cuts of Meat

Because most hearty soups and stews simmer for a lengthy period of time, less expensive cuts of meat can be used—and they'll be quite tender when cooked.

- Beef stew meat is usually cut from the boneless chuck or round sections.
- Pork stew meat is usually cut from the Boston shoulder or picnic shoulder sections.
- Lamb stew meat is usually cut from the shoulder or leg sections or from the neck.
- Veal stew meat is usually cut from the shoulder or leg sections.

Compare the price per pound of these cuts (including the waste) with ready-cut meat. You may find it more economical to cut up the meat yourself.

Chicken-Noodle Soup with Vegetables

2½- to 3-pound broiler-fryer
    chicken, cut up
4 cups water
1 tablespoon salt
1 tablespoon monosodium
    glutamate, if desired
1 teaspoon sugar
¼ teaspoon pepper
3 chicken bouillon cubes
4 medium carrots, cut into ½-inch
    slices (about 2 cups)
4 medium stalks celery, cut into
    ½-inch slices (about 2 cups)
2 cups uncooked thin egg noodles

Remove any excess fat from chicken. Place chicken, giblets (except liver) and neck in Dutch oven. Add remaining ingredients except noodles. Heat to boiling; reduce heat. Cover and simmer until thickest pieces of chicken are done, about 45 minutes.

Cook noodles as directed on package. Remove chicken from broth; cool chicken 10 minutes. Skim fat from broth; strain broth. Remove chicken from bones and skin; cut chicken into bite-size pieces. Add chicken and noodles to broth; heat until hot, about 5 minutes.

5 servings (about 1½ cups each).

Chicken and Barley Soup

2½- to 3-pound broiler-fryer
    chicken, cut up, or 2½ pounds
    chicken pieces
6 cups water
½ cup uncooked regular barley
2 teaspoons instant chicken
    bouillon
2 teaspoons salt
½ teaspoon dried marjoram leaves
½ teaspoon dried thyme leaves
¼ teaspoon pepper
3 medium carrots, cut into ½-inch
    slices (about 1½ cups)
1 medium turnip or rutabaga, cut
    into ¾-inch pieces
1 large onion, coarsely chopped
    (about 1 cup)
1 clove garlic, finely chopped
1 bay leaf
2 medium stalks celery, cut into
    ½-inch slices (about 1 cup)
1 cup frozen green peas

Remove any excess fat from chicken. Place chicken, giblets (except liver) and neck in Dutch oven. Add remaining ingredients except celery and peas. Heat to boiling; reduce heat. Cover and simmer until thickest pieces of chicken are done, about 45 minutes.

Remove chicken from broth; skim fat from broth. Stir celery into broth. Cover and heat to boiling; reduce heat. Simmer until barley is tender, about 15 minutes. Remove chicken from bones and skin; cut chicken into bite-size pieces. Add chicken and peas to soup; heat until hot, about 10 minutes. Remove bay leaf.

8 servings (about 1¼ cups each).

Chicken-Cabbage Soup

5 cups finely chopped cabbage
3 cups cocktail vegetable juice
2 cups water
4 medium carrots, cut into ¼-inch slices (about 2 cups)
2 medium stalks celery, chopped (about 1 cup)
1 medium onion, sliced
2 tablespoons instant chicken bouillon
¼ teaspoon pepper
2½- to 3-pound broiler-fryer chicken
½ teaspoon salt
½ teaspoon paprika
3 tablespoons margarine or butter

Heat cabbage, vegetable juice, water, carrots, celery, onion, bouillon (dry) and pepper to boiling in Dutch oven; reduce heat. Cover and simmer 30 minutes.

Remove bones, skin and any excess fat from chicken. Cut chicken into bite-size pieces; sprinkle with salt and paprika. Cook chicken in margarine until light brown on all sides, 15 to 20 minutes.

Add chicken pieces to soup mixture. Heat to boiling; reduce heat. Cover and simmer until chicken is done, about 30 minutes longer. Serve chicken pieces in soup bowls; pour soup over chicken.

5 servings (about 1½ cups each).

Chicken Gumbo

3- to 4-pound broiler-fryer chicken, cut up
2 cups water or Chicken Broth (page 8)
1 cup chopped celery tops
2 teaspoons salt
1 medium onion, sliced
1 clove garlic, crushed
1 large bay leaf
1 medium onion, chopped (about ½ cup)
1 small green pepper, chopped (about ½ cup)
2 tablespoons margarine or butter
¼ cup snipped parsley
½ teaspoon red pepper sauce
1 can (28 ounces) whole tomatoes, undrained
1½ cups sliced fresh or frozen okra
⅓ cup uncooked long-grain rice
Dash of pepper
1½ teaspoons filé powder

Remove any excess fat from chicken. Heat chicken, giblets (except liver), neck, water, celery tops, salt, sliced onion, garlic and bay leaf to boiling; reduce heat. Cover and simmer until thickest pieces of chicken are done, about 45 minutes.

Remove chicken from broth; cool chicken 10 minutes. Remove chicken from bones and skin; cut chicken into bite-size pieces. Skim fat from broth; strain broth. Place broth and chicken in Dutch oven.

Cook and stir chopped onion and green pepper in margarine until onion is tender. Stir onion mixture, parsley, pepper sauce and tomatoes into chicken and broth; break up tomatoes with fork. Heat to boiling; reduce heat. Simmer uncovered 15 minutes.

Stir in okra, rice and pepper. Heat to boiling; reduce heat. Cover and simmer until rice is done, about 15 minutes. Remove from heat; stir in filé powder. Remove bay leaf. (Soup can be prepared ahead; stir in filé powder after reheating.)

8 servings (about 1½ cups each).

Pictured at right: Chicken Gumbo

Chicken and Leek Soup

2½- to 3-pound broiler-fryer
     chicken, cut up
  4 cups water
  ½ cup regular barley
  2 teaspoons salt
  2 teaspoons instant chicken
     bouillon
  ¼ teaspoon pepper
  1 bay leaf
  1 medium carrot, sliced (about
     ½ cup)
  1 medium stalk celery, sliced
     (about ½ cup)
1½ cups sliced leeks (with tops)

Remove any excess fat from chicken. Heat chicken, giblets (except liver), neck and remaining ingredients except leeks to boiling in Dutch oven; reduce heat. Cover and simmer 30 minutes. Add leeks. Heat to boiling; reduce heat. Cover and simmer until thickest pieces of chicken are done, about 15 minutes.

Remove chicken from broth; cool 10 minutes. Remove chicken from bones and skin; cut chicken into bite-size pieces. Skim fat from broth; remove bay leaf. Add chicken to broth; heat until hot, about 5 minutes.

4 servings (about 1½ cups each).

Buying and Cleaning Leeks

Leeks should have crisp, firm stalks with white bulbs and bright green tops. Small leeks are the most tender and are best served raw (in salads or, marinated, as apppetizers).

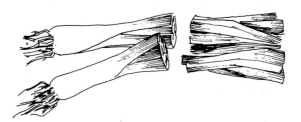

Leeks must be cleaned thoroughly. Trim both ends; remove green tops to within 2 inches of white part.

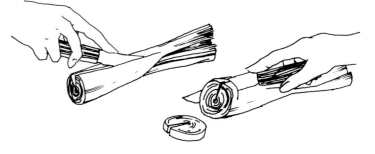

Peel outside layer of bulbs, then cut tops lengthwise but not through. Wash several times in water; drain.

French-style Chicken Soup

2½- to 3-pound broiler-fryer chicken, cut up
2 tablespoons vegetable oil
2 large onions, thinly sliced and separated into rings
2 cloves garlic, finely chopped
1 cup water
1 cup dry white wine or apple juice
1 tablespoon sugar
1 teaspoon salt
1 teaspoon dried thyme leaves
¼ teaspoon pepper
1 can (16 ounces) whole tomatoes, undrained
1 can (10 ¾ ounces) condensed chicken broth
1 medium green pepper, cut into ¼-inch strips
8 slices French bread, toasted
Snipped parsley

Remove skin and any excess fat from chicken pieces. Heat oil in Dutch oven. Cook chicken in oil until brown on all sides; remove chicken from pan. Cook and stir onions and garlic in same pan until onion is tender. Return chicken to pan; add water, wine, sugar, salt, thyme, pepper, tomatoes and broth; break up tomatoes with fork. Heat to boiling; reduce heat. Cover and simmer until chicken is done, about 1 hour.

Skim fat from chicken mixture. Add green pepper. Heat to boiling; reduce heat. Cover and simmer just until green pepper is tender, about 10 minutes. Place a slice of French bread in each serving bowl. Spoon chicken and broth over bread. Sprinkle with parsley.

8 servings (about 1½ cups each).

Mulligatawny Soup

2½- to 3-pound broiler-fryer chicken, cut up
4 cups water
1½ teaspoons salt
1 teaspoon curry powder
1 teaspoon lemon juice
⅛ teaspoon ground cloves
⅛ teaspoon ground mace
1 medium onion, chopped (about ½ cup)
2 tablespoons margarine or butter
2 tablespoons all-purpose flour
2 tomatoes, chopped
1 medium carrot, thinly sliced (about ½ cup)
1 apple, chopped
1 green pepper, cut into ½-inch pieces
Snipped parsley

Remove any excess fat from chicken. Heat chicken, giblets (except liver), neck, water, salt, curry powder, lemon juice, cloves and mace to boiling in Dutch oven; reduce heat. Cover and simmer until thickest pieces of chicken are done, about 45 minutes.

Remove chicken from broth; cool chicken 10 minutes. Remove chicken from bones and skin; cut chicken into bite-size pieces. Skim fat from broth; strain broth. Add enough water to broth, if necessary, to measure 4 cups.

Cook and stir onion in margarine in Dutch oven until tender. Remove from heat; stir in flour. Gradually stir in broth. Add chicken, tomatoes, carrot, apple and green pepper. Heat to boiling; reduce heat. Cover and simmer until carrot is tender, about 10 minutes. Garnish each serving with parsley.

6 servings (about 1¼ cups each).

Chicken Soup with Tortellini

3- to 4-pound broiler-fryer chicken, cut up
6 cups water
2½ teaspoons salt
1 teaspoon peppercorns
1 medium stalk celery (with leaves), cut into 1-inch pieces (about ½ cup)
1 medium carrot, cut into 1-inch pieces (about ½ cup)
1 medium onion, cut into fourths
2 sprigs parsley
1 bay leaf
Tortellini (right)
2 cups water
Snipped parsley
Grated Parmesan cheese

Remove any excess fat from chicken. Place chicken, giblets (except liver) and neck in Dutch oven. Add 6 cups water, the salt, peppercorns, celery, carrot, onion, 2 sprigs parsley and the bay leaf. Heat to boiling; reduce heat. Cover and simmer until thickest pieces of chicken are done, about 45 minutes.

Remove chicken from broth. Strain broth and refrigerate. Cool chicken 10 minutes. Remove chicken from bones and skin. Finely chop enough dark meat to measure ¾ cup; cover and refrigerate. Cut remaining chicken into bite-size pieces and add to broth. Cover and refrigerate. Prepare Tortellini.

Skim fat from broth. Heat broth and 2 cups water to boiling. Add Tortellini. Heat to boiling; reduce heat. Cover and simmer until Tortellini are tender, about 30 minutes. Remove bay leaf. Sprinkle each serving with snipped parsley. Serve with cheese.

8 servings (about 1¼ cups each).

Tortellini

1½ cups all-purpose flour
2 tablespoons water
1 tablespoon olive or vegetable oil
1 teaspoon salt
1 egg
1 egg, separated
2 tablespoons grated Parmesan cheese
⅛ teaspoon grated lemon peel
⅛ teaspoon salt
Dash of ground mace
Dash of pepper

Make a well in center of flour; add water, oil, 1 teaspoon salt, 1 egg and 1 egg white. Stir with fork until mixed; gather dough into a ball. (Sprinkle with a few drops water if dry.) Knead dough on lightly floured board until smooth and elastic, about 5 minutes. Cover and let rest 10 minutes.

Mix reserved ¾ cup chicken, the egg yolk, cheese, lemon peel, ⅛ teaspoon salt, the mace and pepper. Divide dough into halves. Roll one half on lightly floured board into ½-inch square. Cut into twenty 2-inch circles with floured cutter. Place ¼ teaspoon chicken mixture on center of each circle.

Moisten edge of each circle with water. Fold circle in half; press edge with fork to seal. Shape into rings by stretching tips of each half circle slightly; wrap ring around index finger. Moisten one tip with water; gently press tips together. Repeat with remaining dough. Place on tray; cover and refrigerate no longer than 24 hours.

Turkey Soup with Tortellini: Substitute 4-pound turkey hindquarter (drumstick and thigh) for the broiler-fryer chicken.

Do-ahead Tip: Freeze broth and Tortellini separately no longer than 2 weeks. To serve, heat broth and 2 cups water to boiling; continue as directed except simmer 40 minutes.

To make Tortellini, cut the dough into circles, fill with chicken mixture, then fold, seal and shape into crescents.

Chicken-Corn Soup with Rivels

4- to 4½-pound stewing chicken, cut up
12 cups water
2 teaspoons salt
1 teaspoon whole mixed pickling spice
1 medium onion, cut into fourths
1½ cups finely chopped celery (with leaves)
2 cans (17 ounces each) whole kernel corn, undrained
2 teaspoons salt
⅛ teaspoon pepper
2 hard-cooked eggs, peeled and chopped
Rivels (right)

Remove any excess fat from chicken. Heat chicken, giblets (except liver), neck, water, 2 teaspoons salt, the pickling spice and onion to boiling; reduce heat. Cover and simmer until thickest pieces of chicken are done, 2½ to 3 hours. Remove chicken from broth; cool chicken 10 minutes. Remove chicken from bones and skin. Cut chicken into bite-size pieces. Skim fat from broth; strain broth.

Heat broth, chicken, celery and corn to boiling; reduce heat. Simmer uncovered 10 minutes. Stir in 2 teaspoons salt, the pepper, eggs and Rivels. Cover and simmer 7 minutes.

12 servings (about 1½ cups each).

Rivels

Beat 1 egg; mix in 1 cup all-purpose flour and ¼ teaspoon salt until crumbly.

Chicken-Rice Soup with Vegetables

2½ to 3 pounds chicken backs, necks and/or wings
5 cups water
1½ teaspoons salt
1 teaspoon instant chicken bouillon
1 teaspoon chili powder
¼ teaspoon pepper
1 bay leaf
¼ cup uncooked regular rice
2 medium carrots, sliced (about 1 cup)*
2 medium stalks celery, sliced (about 1 cup)*
1 small onion, chopped (¼ cup)
1 can (15½ ounces) kidney beans, undrained
Snipped parsley

Heat chicken, water, salt, bouillon (dry), chili powder, pepper and bay leaf to boiling in Dutch oven; reduce heat. Cover and simmer until chicken is done, 45 to 60 minutes.

Remove chicken from broth; cool chicken 10 minutes. Remove chicken from bones and skin; cut chicken into bite-size pieces. Skim fat from broth; strain broth. Add enough water to broth, if necessary, to measure 5 cups. Heat broth and remaining ingredients except parsley to boiling; reduce heat. Cover and simmer until rice is tender, about 15 minutes. Stir in chicken; heat until hot. Remove bay leaf. Sprinkle with parsley.

5 servings (about 1½ cups each).

*1 package (10 ounces) frozen mixed vegetables (about 2 cups) can be substituted for the carrots and celery.

Au Gratin Chicken Soup

3 cups water
½ cup dry white wine
½ teaspoon dried marjoram leaves
½ teaspoon dried oregano leaves
⅛ teaspoon pepper
1 medium carrot, sliced (about ½ cup)
2 cans (10¾ ounces each) condensed chicken broth
1 package (5.5 ounces) au gratin potato mix
2 cups cut-up cooked chicken (page 8)
1 cup frozen green peas
1 tablespoon snipped parsley
2 medium green onions with tops, sliced

Place water, wine, marjoram, oregano, pepper, carrot, broth, potatoes and Sauce Mix in Dutch oven. Heat to boiling, stirring constantly; reduce heat. Cover and simmer, stirring occasionally, 15 minutes. Stir in chicken, peas, parsley and onions. Cook until vegetables are done, 10 to 15 minutes longer.

6 servings (about 1½ cups each).

Turkey-Rice Soup

1 turkey carcass
8 cups water
2½ teaspoons salt
¼ teaspoon pepper
1 bay leaf
½ cup uncooked brown or regular rice
2 medium stalks celery, chopped (about 1 cup)
1 medium onion, chopped (about ½ cup)
1 carrot, cut into 1-inch pieces
1 can (16 ounces) whole tomatoes, undrained

Break up turkey carcass to fit 8-quart Dutch oven. Add water, salt, pepper and bay leaf. Heat to boiling; reduce heat. Cover and simmer 1½ hours.

Remove bones from broth; cool 10 minutes. Remove turkey from bones; cut turkey into bite-size pieces. Strain broth. Add turkey, rice, celery, onion and carrot to broth in Dutch oven. Heat to boiling; reduce heat. Cover and simmer until rice is tender, about 30 minutes. Stir in tomatoes; break up with fork. Heat until hot. Remove bay leaf.

8 servings (about 1½ cups each).

Fish and Vegetable Soup

1 small cucumber
5 cups Chicken Broth (page 8)
1 tablespoon soy sauce
⅛ teaspoon ground ginger
    Dash of pepper
2 ounces uncooked vermicelli
½ pound fish fillets, cut into ½-inch
    slices
1 can (4¼ ounces) tiny shrimp,
    rinsed and drained
1 cup sliced mushrooms or 1 can
    (4 ounces) mushroom stems
    and pieces, drained
5 cups torn spinach (about
    4 ounces)
¼ cup sliced green onions with tops

Cut cucumber lengthwise into halves; remove seeds. Cut each half crosswise into thin slices. Heat Chicken Broth, soy sauce, ginger and pepper to boiling in 3-quart saucepan; stir in vermicelli. Heat to boiling; cook uncovered just until tender, about 4 minutes. Stir in cucumber, fish, shrimp and mushrooms. Heat to boiling; reduce heat. Simmer uncovered until fish flakes easily with fork, about 1 minute. Stir in spinach until wilted. Sprinkle each serving with green onions.

6 servings (about 1 cup each).

Fish and Lettuce Soup

½ **pound walleye fillets**
1 **teaspoon cornstarch**
2 **teaspoons vegetable oil**
½ **teaspoon salt**
½ **teaspoon soy sauce**
¼ **teaspoon sesame oil**
   Dash of white pepper
½ **head iceberg lettuce**
4 **cups Chicken Broth (page 8)**
1 **teaspoon salt**
1 **green onion with top, chopped**

Cut fish crosswise into ½-inch slices. Toss fish, cornstarch, vegetable oil, ½ teasoon salt, the soy sauce, sesame oil and white pepper in 1-quart glass or plastic bowl. Cover and refrigerate 30 minutes.

Remove core from lettuce; cut lettuce into 8 pieces. Heat Chicken Broth to boiling in 3-quart saucepan. Add lettuce and 1 teaspoon salt; heat to boiling. Stir in fish. Heat to boiling; remove from heat. Stir in green onion.

4 servings (about 1¼ cups each).

Fish Soup Provençale

1½ **cups mayonnaise or salad**
   dressing
3 **cloves garlic, crushed**
½ **cup margarine or butter**
12 **slices French bread**
1 **clove garlic, cut into halves**
1 **pound fish fillets, cut into**
   1-inch pieces
1½ **cups dry white wine**
1 **teaspoon salt**
6 **slices onion**
3 **slices lemon**
5 **sprigs parsley**
1 **bay leaf**
   Paprika

Mix mayonnaise and crushed garlic; cover and refrigerate. Heat ¼ cup of the margarine in 12-inch skillet until melted. Toast 6 of the bread slices in skillet over medium heat until brown on both sides; rub one side of bread with half clove garlic. Remove from skillet; keep warm. Repeat with remaining bread.

Place fish in single layer in skillet. Add wine, salt, onion and lemon slices, parsley, bay leaf and just enough water to cover. Heat to boiling; reduce heat. Simmer uncovered until fish flakes easily with fork, about 6 minutes. Remove fish with slotted spoon; keep warm.

Strain fish broth. Pour 1½ cups of the broth into 2-quart saucepan; gradually beat in mayonnaise mixture. Cook over low heat, stirring constantly, until slightly thickened. Place 2 slices of the French bread upright in each soup bowl; spoon fish between slices. Pour soup over fish; sprinkle with paprika.

6 servings.

Creamy Oriental Tuna Soup

6 cups water
1 tablespoon plus 1 teaspoon soy sauce
½ teaspoon ground ginger
½ teaspoon salt
⅛ teaspoon pepper
1 package (8.75 ounces) main dish mix for creamy noodles and tuna
1 can (6½ ounces) tuna, drained
1 package (6 ounces) frozen pea pods, thawed

Heat water, soy sauce, ginger, salt, pepper, Sauce Mix and Noodles to boiling in Dutch oven, stirring constantly; reduce heat. Cover and simmer, stirring occasionally, 15 minutes; stir in tuna and pea pods. Cover and cook 5 minutes longer.

5 servings (about 1¼ cups each).

Tuna-Zucchini Soup

6 slices bacon
1 medium onion, chopped (about ½ cup)
1 stalk celery, chopped (about ½ cup)
2½ cups Chicken Broth (page 8)
1 cup milk
1 cup shredded Cheddar cheese (about 4 ounces)
¼ teaspoon red pepper sauce
1 can (6½ ounces) tuna in water, drained
1 medium zucchini, shredded (about 1 cup)
1 teaspoon lemon juice

Fry bacon in 3-quart saucepan until crisp. Remove with slotted spoon and drain; crumble and reserve. Remove all but 2 tablespoons bacon fat. Cook and stir onion and celery in bacon fat until onion is tender, about 5 minutes. Stir in Chicken Broth, milk, cheese, pepper sauce and tuna. Heat, stirring occasionally, until tuna is hot and cheese is melted, about 7 minutes. Place 2 cups soup at a time in blender container. Cover and blend on medium speed until smooth, about 15 seconds. Repeat with remaining soup. Stir zucchini and lemon juice into soup; garnish with reserved bacon.

4 servings (about 1½ cups each).

Salmon Gumbo

1 cup diced celery
1 medium onion, chopped (about ½ cup)
½ cup chopped green pepper
1 clove garlic, finely chopped
1 can (16 ounces) okra, drained
2 tablespoons vegetable oil
¼ cup all-purpose flour
2 cups water
2 tablespoons lemon juice
½ teaspoon salt
½ teaspoon dried thyme leaves
¼ teaspoon paprika
⅛ teaspoon red pepper sauce
1 bay leaf
1 can (16 ounces) whole tomatoes, undrained
1 can (16 ounces) salmon, drained and flaked
1½ cups hot cooked rice

Cook and stir celery, onion, green pepper, garlic and okra in oil in 12-inch skillet or Dutch oven until onion is tender, about 5 minutes. Stir in flour. Cook over low heat, stirring constantly, until bubbly; remove from heat. Stir in water. Heat to boiling, stirring constantly. Boil and stir 1 minute. Stir in lemon juice, salt, thyme, paprika, pepper sauce, bay leaf and tomatoes; break up tomatoes with fork. Heat to boiling, stirring constantly. Reduce heat; cover and simmer 20 minutes. Remove bay leaf. Stir in salmon; heat until hot. Top each serving with rice. Serve with additional red pepper sauce if desired.

5 servings (about 1½ cups each).

Seafood in Your Soups and Stews

Fish is an excellent source of protein. Only 2 to 3 ounces of fish or shellfish—not counting bones or shells—supply as much protein as you need at one meal. This adds up to about one-fourth of the estimated adult daily protein requirement.

The servings in these recipes are based on protein needs per meal. They may seem small for more robust appetites. If so, either assume fewer servings per recipes or increase the amount or variety of foods you serve with the soup or stew.

Shrimp Gumbo

2 onions, sliced
½ green pepper, thinly sliced
2 cloves garlic, finely chopped
¼ cup margarine or butter
2 tablespoons all-purpose flour
3 cups Beef Broth (page 6)
1 tablespoon plus 1½ teaspoons salt
1 tablespoon plus 1 teaspoon Worcestershire sauce
½ teaspoon chili powder
¼ teaspoon pepper
⅛ teaspoon ground cloves
1 bay leaf
    Pinch of dried basil leaves
1 can (16 ounces) okra, drained, or 1 package (10 ounces) frozen okra
1 can (16 ounces) whole tomatoes, undrained
1 can (6 ounces) tomato paste
1½ pounds fresh or frozen raw shrimp
3 cups hot cooked rice
¼ cup snipped parsley

Cook and stir onions, green pepper and garlic in margarine in Dutch oven over low heat until onions are tender. Stir in flour. Cook over low heat, stirring constantly, until bubbly; remove from heat. Stir in Beef Broth, salt, Worcestershire sauce, chili powder, pepper, cloves, bay leaf, basil, okra, tomatoes and tomato paste; break up tomatoes with fork. Simmer uncovered 45 minutes.

Peel shrimp. (If shrimp is frozen, do not thaw; peel under running cold water.) Make a shallow cut lengthwise down back of each shrimp; wash out sand vein. Stir shrimp into tomato mixture. Cover and simmer until shrimp are pink and tender, about 5 minutes. Remove bay leaf. Mix rice and parsley; serve with gumbo.

10 servings (about 1¼ cups each).

Crabmeat-Vegetable Soup

1 medium onion, chopped (about ½ cup)
1 clove garlic, crushed
1 tablespoon margarine or butter
1 large tomato, peeled and chopped
3 cups Fish Broth (page 8)
2 tablespoons snipped parsley
½ teaspoon salt
3 drops red pepper sauce
4 new potatoes, cut in half
1 package (10 ounces) frozen whole-kernel corn
1½ cups cooked crabmeat

Cook and stir onion and garlic in margarine in 3-quart saucepan until onion is tender. Stir in tomato; cook 2 minutes. Stir in broth, parsley, salt, pepper sauce, potatoes and corn. Heat to boiling; reduce heat. Cover and simmer until potatoes are tender, about 10 minutes. Stir in crabmeat. Heat 2 minutes. *(Pictured on page 7.)*

4 servings (about 1½ cups each).

Black Bean Soup

3 cups water
4 ounces dried black beans (about ½ cup)
1 ham bone or 1 pound ham shank or smoked pork hocks
½ teaspoon salt
1 clove garlic, finely chopped
1 small bay leaf
½ small dried hot pepper, crumbled
1 medium carrot, sliced (about ½ cup)
1 medium stalk celery, chopped (about ½ cup)
1 medium onion, chopped (about ½ cup)
2 tablespoons chopped red onion
3 lemon slices
3 hard-cooked eggs, shredded
Dry white wine, if desired

Heat water and beans to boiling in Dutch oven; boil 2 minutes. Remove from heat; cover and let stand 1 hour.

Add ham bone. Heat to boiling; reduce heat. Cover and simmer until beans are tender, about 2 hours (do not boil or beans will burst). Skim fat. Stir in salt, garlic, bay leaf, hot pepper, carrot, celery and ½ cup onion. Cover and simmer 1 hour.

Remove ham bone and bay leaf. (Soup can be placed in blender container; cover and blend until uniform consistency.) Trim ham from bone and stir into soup. Serve with chopped red onion, lemon slices and shredded eggs. (The wine can be stirred into soup.)

6 servings (about 1 cup each).

Stormy Day Bean Soup

7 cups water
1 pound dried navy beans (about 2 cups)
2 cups cubed cooked smoked ham
1 small onion, chopped (about ¼ cup)
½ teaspoon salt
Dash of pepper
1 bay leaf
1 ham bone

Heat water and beans to boiling in Dutch oven; boil 2 minutes. Remove from heat; cover and let stand 1 hour.

Stir in cubed ham, onion, salt, pepper and bay leaf; add ham bone. Heat to boiling; reduce heat. Cover and simmer, skimming foam occasionally, until beans are tender, about 1¼ hours. Add water during cooking if necessary.

Remove bay leaf and ham bone; remove ham from bone. Trim excess fat from ham; cut ham into ½-inch pieces. Stir ham into soup.

4 servings (about 1½ cups each).

Calico Bean Soup

8 cups water
   Bean Soup Mix (right)
2 medium carrots, chopped (about
   1 cup)
2 stalks celery, chopped (about
   1 cup)
2 pounds smoked ham shanks, ham
   hocks or 1 ham bone

Heat water and Bean Soup Mix to boiling in Dutch oven; boil 2 minutes. Remove from heat; cover and let stand 1 hour.

Stir in carrots and celery; add ham shanks. Heat to boiling; reduce heat. Cover and simmer until beans are tender, about 2 hours. Skim fat if necessary.

Remove ham shanks; remove ham from bone. Trim excess fat from ham; cut ham into ½-inch pieces. Stir ham into soup. Heat until hot.

6 servings (about 1½ cups each).

Bean Soup Mix

2 cups mixed dried beans (⅓ cup
   each of yellow split peas, green
   split peas, lima beans, pinto
   beans, kidney beans and great
   northern beans)
¼ cup instant minced onion
2 teaspoons instant chicken
   bouillon
¼ teaspoon ground cumin
¼ teaspoon garlic powder

Combine all ingredients.

Do-ahead Tip: Prepare several packages of Bean Soup Mix and store in plastic bag or airtight container in a cool, dry place. Use 1 soup mix package for each recipe of Calico Bean Soup.

Northern Bean Soup

8 cups water
1 pound dried great northern or
    lima beans (about 2 cups)
1 tablespoon instant beef bouillon
1 teaspoon salt
½ teaspoon pepper
1 large onion, chopped (about
    1 cup)
1 clove garlic, crushed
1 can (8 ounces) tomato sauce
2¼ pounds smoked pork hocks
2 cups mashed potatoes
2 medium carrots, cut into ½-inch
    pieces (about 1 cup)
2 medium stalks celery, cut into
    ½-inch pieces (about 1 cup)

Heat water and beans to boiling in Dutch oven; boil 2 minutes. Remove from heat; cover and let stand 1 hour.

Stir bouillon (dry), salt, pepper, onion, garlic and tomato sauce into beans; add pork hocks. Heat to boiling; reduce heat. Cover and simmer until beans are tender, about 2 hours (do not boil or beans will burst). Skim fat.

Remove pork hocks; remove pork from bone. Trim excess fat from pork; cut pork into ½-inch pieces. Stir pork, potatoes, carrots and celery into soup. Heat to boiling; reduce heat. Cover and simmer until vegetables are tender, about 45 minutes. Stir in 1 to 2 cups milk or water for thinner consistency.

8 servings (about 1½ cups each).

Bean and Sausage Soup

7 cups water
1 pound dried great northern or
    lima beans (about 2 cups)
1 teaspoon salt
½ teaspoon pepper
1 large onion, chopped (about 1 cup)
2 cloves garlic, finely chopped
1 can (16 ounces) whole tomatoes,
    undrained
1 pound kielbasa or Polish sausage,
    cut into ¼-inch slices
2 medium carrots, cut into ¼-inch
    slices (about 1 cup)
2 medium stalks celery, cut into
    ¼-inch slices (about 1 cup)

Heat water and beans to boiling in Dutch oven; boil 2 minutes. Remove from heat; cover and let stand 1 hour.

Add salt, pepper, onion, garlic and tomatoes; break up tomatoes with fork. Heat to boiling; reduce heat. Cover and simmer until beans are tender, about 2 hours (do not boil or beans will burst). Skim fat if necessary.

Cook sausage over medium heat until brown; drain. Stir sausage, carrots and celery into bean mixture. Heat to boiling; reduce heat. Cover and simmer until vegetables are tender, about 30 minutes. Stir in small amount of milk or water for thinner consistency.

8 servings (about 1¼ cups each).

Minestrone

1 cup water
½ cup dried great northern, navy or
    kidney beans
4 cups Chicken Broth (page 8)
½ cup uncooked macaroni
1 tablespoon snipped parsley
1 teaspoon salt
½ teaspoon dried basil leaves
⅛ teaspoon pepper
1 bay leaf
2 medium carrots, sliced (about
    1 cup)
1 stalk celery, sliced (about ½ cup)
1 medium onion, chopped (about
    ½ cup)
2 small tomatoes, chopped
1 clove garlic, chopped
4 ounces green beans, cut into
    1-inch pieces (about ¾ cup)
2 small zucchini, cut into 1-inch
    slices
    Grated Parmesan cheese

Heat water and dried beans to boiling in Dutch oven; boil 2 minutes. Remove from heat. Cover and let stand 1 hour.

Add enough water to cover beans if necessary. Heat to boiling; reduce heat. Cover and simmer until tender, 1 to 1½ hours (do not boil or beans will burst).

Add remaining ingredients except green beans, zucchini and cheese to dried bean mixture. Heat to boiling; reduce heat. Cover and simmer 15 minutes. Add green beans and zucchini. Heat to boiling; reduce heat. Cover and simmer until macaroni and vegetables are tender, 10 to 15 minutes. Remove bay leaf. Serve with cheese.

5 servings (about 1¼ cups each).

Garbanzo Bean Soup

8 cups water
1 pound dried garbanzo beans
    (about 2½ cups)
1 tablespoon instant beef bouillon
1 teaspoon salt
¼ teaspoon pepper
⅛ teaspoon cayenne pepper
1 large onion, chopped (about
    1 cup)
2 cloves garlic, chopped
1½ to 2 pounds smoked ham shanks
    or 1 ham bone
3 medium potatoes, cut into cubes
    (about 3 cups)
1 small head cabbage (about
    1 pound), coarsely chopped
    (about 6 cups)

Heat water and beans to boiling in Dutch oven; boil 2 minutes. Remove from heat; cover and let stand 1 hour.

Stir in bouillon (dry), salt, pepper, cayenne, onion and garlic; add ham shanks. Heat to boiling; reduce heat. Cover and simmer until beans are almost tender, 1½ to 2 hours (do not boil or beans will burst). Skim fat if necessary.

Remove ham shanks; cool slightly. Remove ham from bone. Trim excess fat from ham; cut ham into ½-inch pieces. Stir ham, potatoes and cabbage into soup. Heat to boiling; reduce heat. Cover and simmer until beans and potatoes are tender, about 30 minutes.

8 servings (about 1½ cups each).

Chili-Bean Soup

1 medium onion, sliced
1 large clove garlic, crushed
2 tablespoons margarine or butter
1 tablespoon chili powder
¼ teaspoon ground coriander
1 can (28 ounces) whole tomatoes, undrained
1 can (20 ounces) kidney beans, drained
1 can (16 ounces) pinto beans, drained
1 can (4 ounces) chopped green chilies, drained
½ cup shredded Cheddar cheese (about 2 ounces)
1 cup shredded Monterey Jack cheese (about 4 ounces)

Cook and stir onion and garlic in margarine in 3-quart saucepan until onion is tender, about 5 minutes. Stir in chili powder, coriander, tomatoes, kidney beans, pinto beans and chilies. Break up tomatoes with fork. Heat to boiling; reduce heat. Cover and simmer 30 minutes. Stir in Cheddar cheese and ½ cup of the Monterey Jack cheese; stir over low heat until cheese is melted. Sprinkle each serving with remaining cheese.

4 servings (about 1½ cups each).

Lentil-Spinach Soup

2 medium onions, sliced
1 clove garlic, finely chopped
2 tablespoons olive or vegetable oil
3 cups water
8 ounces dried lentils (about 1¼ cups)
1 teaspoon salt
10 ounces spinach,* chopped
1 teaspoon grated lemon peel
2 teaspoons lemon juice

Cook and stir onions and garlic in oil in 3-quart saucepan over medium heat until onions are tender. Stir in water, lentils and salt. Heat to boiling; reduce heat. Cover and simmer 1 hour. Stir in spinach, lemon peel and lemon juice. Cover and simmer until spinach is tender, about 5 minutes.

4 servings (about 1¼ cups each).

*1 package (10 ounces) frozen chopped spinach, thawed, can be substituted for the fresh spinach.

Split Pea Soup

8 cups water
1 pound dried split peas (about 2¼ cups)
1 large onion, chopped (about 1 cup)
1 cup finely chopped celery
¼ teaspoon pepper
2 pounds ham shanks, ham hocks or ham bone
3 medium carrots, cut into ¼-inch slices (about 1½ cups)

Heat water and peas to boiling in Dutch oven; boil 2 minutes. Remove from heat; cover and let stand 1 hour.

Stir in onion, celery and pepper; add ham shanks. Heat to boiling; reduce heat. Cover and simmer until peas are tender, about 1½ hours. Skim fat if necessary.

Remove ham shanks; remove ham from bone. Trim excess fat from ham; cut ham into ½-inch pieces. Stir ham and carrots into soup. Heat to boiling; reduce heat. Cover and simmer until carrots are tender and soup is desired consistency, about 30 minutes.

8 servings (about 1½ cups each).

Split Pea and Chicken Soup

4 cups water
½ pound dried split peas (about 1¼ cups)
1 teaspoon salt
½ teaspoon chili powder
¼ teaspoon ground turmeric
¼ teaspoon ground cumin
¼ teaspoon ground ginger
⅛ teaspoon pepper
2 medium carrots, sliced (about 1 cup)
2 medium stalks celery, sliced (about 1 cup)
1 medium onion, chopped (about ½ cup)
1 clove garlic, chopped
1½ cups cut-up cooked chicken (page 8)
1 medium tomato, chopped (about 1 cup)

Heat water and peas to boiling in Dutch oven; boil 2 minutes. Remove from heat; cover and let stand 1 hour.

Stir remaining ingredients except chicken and tomato into peas. Heat to boiling; reduce heat. Cover and simmer until beans are tender, about 45 minutes. Add chicken and tomato; heat to boiling. Garnish each serving with spoonful of dairy sour cream if desired.

4 servings (about 1½ cups each).

Chicken-Broccoli Chowder

2 cups Chicken Broth (page 8)
⅓ cup chopped onion
1 package (10 ounces) frozen chopped broccoli
1⅓ cups mashed potato mix
2 cups cut-up cooked chicken (page 8)
2 cups shredded Swiss cheese (about 8 ounces)
2 cups milk
½ teaspoon salt

Heat Chicken Broth, onion and broccoli to boiling in 3-quart saucepan. Reduce heat; cover and simmer 5 minutes. Stir in potatoes until well blended. Stir in remaining ingredients. Heat over low heat, stirring occasionally, until hot and cheese is melted, about 5 minutes. *(Pictured on page 7.)*

6 servings (about 1⅓ cups each).

Quick Ham and Cauliflower Chowder

2½ cups water
½ cup chopped cauliflower
⅛ teaspoon dry mustard
Dash of pepper
1 package (5.25 ounces) scalloped potato mix
1 can (10¾ ounces) condensed chicken broth
1 cup diced fully cooked smoked ham
1 cup half-and-half

Mix water, cauliflower, mustard, pepper, potatoes, Sauce Mix and broth in 3-quart saucepan. Heat to boiling, stirring frequently; reduce heat. Cover and simmer, stirring occasionally, until potatoes are tender, 25 minutes. Stir in ham and half-and-half. Cook uncovered just until hot, about 5 minutes longer (do not boil). Garnish with snipped parsley if desired.

4 servings (about 1¼ cups each).

Sausage Chowder

1 package (12 ounces) smoked sausage links, cut into ½-inch slices
1 small green pepper, chopped (about ½ cup)
1 small onion, chopped (about ¼ cup)
1 tablespoon margarine or butter
⅔ cup milk
1 can (16½ ounces) cream-style corn
1 can (10¾ ounces) condensed cream of potato soup

Cook and stir sausage, green pepper and onion in margarine in 3-quart saucepan over medium heat until sausage is brown. Stir in remaining ingredients; heat just until hot (do not boil).

4 servings (about 1¼ cups each).

Fish Chowder

1 cup water
1 pound haddock or cod
¼ pound lean salt pork, diced
1 medium onion, sliced
1 teaspoon salt
¼ teaspoon pepper
1 small bay leaf
1 large potato, pared and diced
1 stalk celery, chopped (about
    ½ cup)
2 cups milk
1 tablespoon margarine or butter

Heat water to boiling. Add fish; reduce heat. Cover and simmer 15 minutes. Drain, reserving broth. Remove bones from fish. Cook and stir salt pork in 3-quart saucepan over low heat until pork is crisp and onion is tender. Remove pork with slotted spoon and drain; reserve.

Cook and stir onion in pork fat over low heat until golden brown. Stir in fish, salt, pepper, bay leaf, potato and celery. Add enough boiling water to reserved broth to measure 1½ cups. Stir into fish mixture. Cover and simmer 30 minutes. Stir in milk and margarine; simmer uncovered 5 minutes. Remove bay leaf. Sprinkle each serving with reserved salt pork.

6 servings (about 1 cup each).

Cheesy Tuna-Corn Chowder

6 cups water
2 tablespoons grated Parmesan
    cheese
¼ teaspoon salt
⅛ teaspoon pepper
1 can (12 ounces) whole kernel corn
    with sweet peppers, undrained
1 package (7.25 ounces) main dish
    mix for noodles, cheese sauce
    and tuna
1 can (6½ ounces) tuna, drained
2 tablespoons snipped parsley

Heat water, cheese, salt, pepper, corn and Sauce Mix to boiling in Dutch oven, stirring constantly; reduce heat. Cover and simmer, stirring occasionally, 10 minutes; stir in Noodles and tuna. Cover and cook 10 minutes longer; stir in parsley. Serve with additional cheese if desired.

5 servings (about 1½ cups each).

New England Clam Chowder

¼ cup cut-up bacon or lean salt pork
1 medium onion, chopped (about
  ½ cup)
2 cans (8 ounces each) minced or
  whole clams, drained (reserve
  liquid)*
1 cup finely chopped potato
½ teaspoon salt
  Dash of pepper
2 cups milk

Cook and stir bacon and onion in 2-quart saucepan until bacon is crisp and onion is tender. Add enough water, if necessary, to reserved clam liquid to measure 1 cup. Stir clams, liquid, potato, salt and pepper into onion mixture. Heat to boiling. Cover and cook until potato is tender, about 15 minutes. Stir in milk. Heat, stirring occasionally, just until hot (do not boil).

4 servings (about 1 cup each).

*1 pint shucked fresh clams with liquid can be substituted for the canned clams. Chop clams and add with the potatoes.

Manhattan Clam Chowder

¼ cup finely cut-up lean salt pork or
  bacon or margarine or butter
1 small onion, finely chopped
  (about ¼ cup)
2 cans (8 ounces each) minced or
  whole clams, drained (reserve
  liquid)*
2 cups finely chopped potatoes
1 cup water
⅓ cup chopped celery
2 teaspoons snipped parsley
1 teaspoon salt
¼ teaspoon dried thyme leaves
⅛ teaspoon pepper
1 can (16 ounces) whole tomatoes,
  undrained

Cook and stir salt pork and onion in Dutch oven until pork is crisp and onion is tender. Drain clams, reserving liquid. Stir clam liquid, potatoes, water and celery into onion and pork. Cover and cook until potatoes are tender, about 10 minutes. Stir in clams, and the remaining ingredients. Break up tomatoes with fork. Heat to boiling, stirring occasionally.

5 servings (about 1½ cups each).

*1 pint shucked fresh clams with liquid can be substituted for the canned clams. Chop clams and add with the potatoes.

Pictured at left: New England Clam Chowder (top) and Manhattan Clam Chowder

Corn-Tomato Chowder

¼ pound bacon, cut into 2-inch
  pieces
1 small onion, diced (about ¼ cup)
2 cups diced potatoes
1 tablespoon sugar
2 teaspoons salt
½ teaspoon paprika
⅛ teaspoon pepper
1 can (16 ounces) whole kernel corn,
  undrained
1 can (16 ounces) tomatoes,
  undrained
3 cups water
1 cup evaporated milk

Fry bacon in 3-quart saucepan or Dutch oven until golden brown. Add onion; cook and stir over low heat 5 minutes. Stir in potatoes, sugar, salt, paprika, pepper, corn and tomatoes; break up tomatoes with fork. Add water. Heat to boiling; reduce heat. Cover and simmer until potatoes are tender, 20 to 25 minutes. Remove from heat; gradually stir in milk.

7 servings (about ½ cup each).

Cheesy Vegetable Chowder

2 cups water
1 teaspoon salt
3 medium carrots, sliced (about
  1 cup)
2 stalks celery, chopped (about
  ½ cup)
1 small onion, chopped (about
  ¼ cup)
½ cup margarine or butter
½ cup all-purpose flour
½ teaspoon pepper
2 cups milk
1 can (8¾ ounces) whole kernel
  corn, drained, or 1 cup frozen
  whole kernel corn
1 can (8½ ounces) green peas,
  drained, or 1 cup frozen green
  peas
1 can (4 ounces) mushroom stems
  and pieces, drained
6 slices bacon, crisply fried and
  crumbled
4 ounces Swiss or American cheese,
  cut into ½-inch cubes

Heat water to boiling in 3-quart saucepan. Stir in salt, carrots, celery and onion. Heat to boiling; reduce heat. Cover and simmer until vegetables are tender, about 10 minutes. Heat margarine in 2-quart saucepan over low heat until melted; stir in flour and pepper. Heat to boiling over medium heat, stirring constantly. Remove from heat; gradually stir in milk. Heat to boiling, stirring constantly; boil and stir 1 minute. Stir milk mixture, corn, peas, mushrooms and bacon into carrot mixture; heat until hot. Stir in cheese; heat until cheese begins to melt. Top each serving with croutons if desired.

7 servings (about 1¼ cups each).

Stews

*Savory rib-sticking stews have many virtues:
They can be prepared ahead of time, they're great
for entertaining, they even travel for picnic fare.
Best of all, when time and money have to be budgeted,
a meal-in-a-dish is the matter-of-fact solution.*

Tomato-Beef Stew with Biscuits

2 pounds beef stew meat, cut into
    1-inch pieces
2 medium onions, chopped (about
    1 cup)
2 tablespoons vegetable oil
2½ cups hot water
1 tablespoon sugar
1½ teaspoons salt
¼ teaspoon pepper
1 can (16 ounces) whole tomatoes,
    undrained
1 can (6 ounces) tomato paste
1 can (4 ounces) mushroom stems
    and pieces, undrained
1 cup thinly sliced carrots
2 medium stalks celery, cut into
    slices (about 1 cup)
½ teaspoon dried thyme leaves
¼ teaspoon dried marjoram leaves
1 bay leaf
¼ cup cold water
2 tablespoons all-purpose flour
  Sour Cream Biscuits (right)

Cook and stir beef and onions in oil in Dutch oven until beef is brown. Stir in hot water, sugar, salt, pepper, tomatoes, tomato paste and mushrooms. Heat to boiling, stirring occasionally; reduce heat. Cover and simmer, stirring occasionally, until beef is almost tender, about 1½ hours.

Add carrots, celery, thyme, marjoram and bay leaf. Cover and simmer 30 minutes. Remove bay leaf. Mix cold water and flour until smooth; gradually stir into beef mixture. Heat to boiling, stirring constantly. Boil and stir 1 minute; reduce heat.

Heat oven to 450°. Prepare Sour Cream Biscuits. Drop dough by spoonfuls onto hot beef mixture. Bake until biscuits are brown, about 10 minutes.

5 or 6 servings.

Sour Cream Biscuits

2 cups buttermilk baking mix
⅓ cup margarine or butter, melted
1 cup dairy sour cream

Mix all ingredients until soft dough forms; beat vigorously 20 strokes.

Savory Beef Stew with Dumplings

½ cup all-purpose flour
2 to 3 teaspoons salt
¼ teaspoon pepper
2 pounds beef stew meat, cut into
   1-inch pieces
3 tablespoons vegetable oil
4 cups water
4 cups ¾-inch cubes potatoes
2 tablespoons snipped parsley
½ teaspoon dried thyme leaves
1 bay leaf
3 medium carrots, cut into ¼-inch
   slices (about 1½ cups)
2 medium stalks celery, cut into
   ¼-inch slices (about 1 cup)
2 medium onions, sliced
   Herb Dumplings (right)

Mix flour, salt and pepper; coat beef. Heat oil in Dutch oven until hot; add beef and remaining flour mixture. Cook and stir until beef is brown. Add water. Heat to boiling; reduce heat. Cover and simmer 1½ hours. Add remaining ingredients except Herb Dumplings. Cover and simmer 30 minutes. Remove bay leaf.

Prepare Herb Dumplings. Drop dough by spoonfuls onto hot beef or vegetables (do not drop directly into liquid). Cook uncovered low heat 10 minutes. Cover and cook 10 minutes longer.

6 to 8 servings.

Herb Dumplings

3 tablespoons shortening
1½ cups all-purpose flour
2 teaspoons baking powder
¾ teaspoon salt
¼ teaspoon dried sage leaves
¼ teaspoon dried thyme leaves
¾ cup milk

Cut shortening into flour, baking powder, salt, sage and thyme until mixture resembles fine crumbs. Stir in milk.

Autumn Stew

¼ cup all-purpose flour
1½ teaspoons salt
¼ teaspoon paprika
¼ teaspoon pepper
1½ pounds beef stew meat, cut into
   1-inch pieces
2 tablespoons shortening
2 cups water
1 teaspoon pumpkin pie spice
2 beef bouillon cubes
1 medium onion, chopped (about
   ½ cup)
1 clove garlic, finely chopped
1 can (16 ounces) stewed tomatoes
2½ cups 1-inch cubes pumpkin or
   Hubbard squash
3 medium potatoes, pared and cut
   into 1-inch cubes

Mix flour, salt, paprika and pepper; coat beef with flour mixture. Cook and stir beef in shortening in Dutch oven until brown. Stir in remaining ingredients except pumpkin and potatoes. Heat to boiling; reduce heat. Cover and simmer until beef is almost tender, about 2 hours. Stir in pumpkin and potatoes. Cover and simmer until vegetables are tender, about 30 minutes.

4 servings.

Hungarian Goulash

2 pounds beef stew meat, cut into
   1-inch pieces
1 cup sliced onion
⅛ teaspoon instant minced garlic
¼ cup shortening
1½ cups water
¾ cup catsup
2 tablespoons Worcestershire
   sauce
1 tablespoon packed brown sugar
2 teaspoons salt
2 teaspoons paprika
½ teaspoon dry mustard
   Dash cayenne pepper
¼ cup cold water
2 tablespoons all-purpose flour
   Noodles (right)

Cook and stir beef, onion and garlic in shortening in 12-inch skillet until beef is brown and onion is tender. Drain fat. Stir in 1½ cups water, the catsup, Worcestershire sauce, brown sugar, salt, paprika, mustard and cayenne pepper. Cover and simmer 2 to 2½ hours.

Shake ¼ cup cold water and the flour in tightly covered container; gradually stir into beef mixture. Heat to boiling, stirring constantly. Boil and stir 1 minute. Serve over hot Noodles.

6 to 8 servings.

Noodles

Drop 8 ounces uncooked noodles into 6 cups rapidly boiling salted water (4 teaspoons salt). Heat to rapid boiling. Cook, stirring constantly, 3 minutes. Cover tightly. Remove from heat and let stand 10 minutes; drain.

Ragout Mignon

1½ pounds beef chuck or bottom round, cut into 2-inch pieces
1 teaspoon salt
¼ teaspoon pepper
2 tablespoons shortening
1 small onion, chopped (about ¼ cup)
1 carrot, chopped
1 stalk celery, chopped
1 clove garlic, finely chopped
¼ cup all-purpose flour
2 cups water
¼ teaspoon dried thyme leaves
¼ teaspoon dried sage leaves
3 sprigs parsley
1 bay leaf
1 can (8½ ounces) whole tomatoes, undrained
6 small onions
4 medium potatoes, cut into fourths
3 carrots, halved lengthwise and crosswise
1 teaspoon salt

Sprinkle beef with 1 teaspoon salt and the pepper. Cook and stir beef in shortening in 12-inch skillet until brown; reduce heat. Add chopped onion, chopped carrot, chopped celery and the garlic. Cook until onion is light brown. Stir in flour; cook over low heat, stirring constantly, until bubbly; remove from heat. Stir in water. Heat to boiling, stirring constantly. Stir in thyme, sage, parsley, bay leaf and tomatoes; break up tomatoes with fork. Cover and simmer 1 hour.

Add onions, potatoes and carrots; sprinkle with 1 teaspoon salt. Heat to boiling; reduce heat. Cover and simmer 1½ to 2 hours, or until beef is tender. Remove bay leaf.

6 servings.

French Boiled Dinner

1½-pound beef boneless chuck roast*
1 marrow bone, if desired
4 cups water
1 teaspoon salt
¼ teaspoon dried thyme leaves
8 peppercorns
1 bay leaf
1½ pounds chicken drumsticks
10 to 12 small carrots
10 to 12 small onions or 3 large onions, cut into fourths
3 medium turnips, cut into fourths
4 stalks celery, cut into 1-inch pieces
¾ teaspoon salt
⅛ teaspoon pepper

Place beef, marrow bone, water, 1 teaspoon salt, the thyme, peppercorns and bay leaf in Dutch oven. Add water. Heat to boiling; reduce heat. Cover and simmer 1 hour. Add chicken; cover and simmer 1 hour longer.

Add carrots, onions, turnips, and celery; sprinkle with ¾ teaspoon salt and the pepper. Cover and simmer until beef and vegetables are tender, about 45 minutes. Remove chicken and vegetables to warm platter; slice beef. Strain broth; serve as first course.

10 to 12 servings.

*A 3-pound beef boneless chuck roast can be substituted for the 1½-pound roast and the chicken.

Spanish Boiled Dinner

1½-pound beef boneless brisket or
     beef boneless chuck, tip or
     round
1 beef soup bone (about 1 pound)
8 cups water
2½ teaspoons salt
¼ teaspoon pepper
1 medium onion, chopped (about
     ½ cup)
2 cloves garlic, chopped
1 bay leaf
1 pound chorizo sausage, cut into
     ½-inch pieces
3 medium carrots, sliced (about
     1½ cups)
3 medium stalks celery, sliced
     (about 1½ cups)
1 small head cabbage, cut into
     8 wedges
1 can (about 16 ounces) garbanzo
     beans, undrained

Trim excess fat from beef. Heat beef, soup bone, water, salt, pepper, onion, garlic and bay leaf to boiling in Dutch oven; reduce heat. Cover and simmer 1½ hours.

Cook sausage over medium heat, turning carefully, about 5 minutes; drain. Remove soup bone from broth. Add sausage, carrots, celery, cabbage and garbanzo beans to broth. Heat to boiling; reduce heat. Cover and simmer until beef and vegetables are tender, 30 to 40 minutes.

Remove beef from broth; cut into slices. Remove sausage and vegetables with slotted spoon. Arrange meat and vegetables on heated platter. Serve broth as first course, or serve vegetable mixture and broth together.

8 servings.

Burgundy Beef Stew

6 slices bacon, cut into 1-inch
     pieces
2-pound beef boneless chuck eye,
     rolled rump roast or bottom
     round roast, cut into 1-inch
     pieces
½ cup all-purpose flour
1½ cups dry red wine
1¼ teaspoons salt
1 teaspoon instant beef bouillon
½ teaspoon dried thyme leaves
¼ teaspoon pepper
1 clove garlic, chopped
1 bay leaf
8 ounces mushrooms, sliced
4 medium onions, sliced
2 tablespoons margarine or butter
     Snipped parsley
     French bread

Fry bacon in Dutch oven over medium heat until crisp. Remove bacon; drain and reserve. Coat beef with flour; cook and stir beef in hot bacon fat until brown. Drain excess fat from Dutch oven. Add wine and just enough water to cover beef. Stir in salt, bouillon (dry), thyme, pepper, garlic and bay leaf. Heat to boiling; reduce heat. Cover and simmer until beef is tender, about 1½ hours.

Cook and stir mushrooms and onions in margarine over medium heat until onions are tender. Stir mushrooms, onions and bacon into stew. Cover and simmer 10 minutes. Remove bay leaf. Garnish with parsley. Serve with French bread.

8 servings.

Easy Burgundy Stew

2 pounds beef boneless bottom or
  top round, tip or chuck steak,
  cut into 1-inch pieces
4 medium carrots, sliced (about
  2 cups)
2 medium stalks celery, sliced
  (about 1 cup)
2 medium onions, sliced
1 can (8 ounces) water chestnuts,
  sliced
1 can (8 ounces) mushroom stems
  and pieces, drained
3 tablespoons all-purpose flour
1 teaspoon salt
1 teaspoon dried thyme leaves
1 teaspoon dry mustard
¼ teaspoon pepper
1 cup water
1 cup dry red wine*
1 can (16 ounces) whole tomatoes,
  undrained

Mix beef, carrots, celery, onions, water chestnuts and mushrooms in Dutch oven or 4-quart casserole. Mix flour, salt, thyme, mustard and pepper; stir into beef mixture. Stir in remaining ingredients. Break up tomatoes with fork. Cover and bake in 325° oven until beef is tender and stew is thickened, about 4 hours.

8 servings.

*1 cup Beef Broth (page 6) can be substituted for the wine.

Beef and Beer Stew

1½-pound beef boneless chuck or
round steak, 1 inch thick
¼ pound bacon
4 medium onions, sliced
1 clove garlic, chopped
3 tablespoons all-purpose flour
1 cup water
1 tablespoon packed brown sugar
2 teaspoons salt
½ teaspoon dried thyme leaves
¼ teaspoon pepper
1 bay leaf
1 can (12 or 16 ounces) beer
1 tablespoon vinegar
Snipped parsley
Noodles (right)

Cut beef across grain into ½-inch slices; cut slices into 2-inch strips. (For ease in cutting, freeze beef until partially frozen, about 1½ hours.) Cut bacon into ¼-inch pieces; fry in Dutch oven until crisp. Remove bacon; drain and reserve. Pour off fat and reserve. Cook and stir onions and garlic in 2 tablespoons of the reserved bacon fat until tender, about 10 minutes. Remove onions. Cook and stir beef in remaining bacon fat until brown, about 15 minutes.

Stir in flour to coat beef; gradually stir in water. Add onions, brown sugar, salt, thyme, pepper, bay leaf and beer. Add just enough water to cover beef mixture, if necessary. Heat to boiling; reduce heat. Cover and simmer until beef is tender, 1 to 1½ hours. Remove bay leaf. Stir in vinegar; sprinkle with bacon and parsley. Serve with hot Noodles.

6 servings.

Noodles

Drop 8 ounces uncooked noodles into 6 cups rapidly boiling salted water (4 teaspoons salt). Heat to rapid boiling. Cook, stirring constantly, 3 minutes. Cover tightly. Remove from heat and let stand 10 minutes; drain.

Cube Steak Stew

3 tablespoons all-purpose flour
1½ teaspoons salt
½ teaspoon monosodium
glutamate, if desired
¼ teaspoon pepper
4 beef cube steaks, cut into
2 x ½-inch strips
3 tablespoons shortening
1 teaspoon salt
4 medium potatoes, cut into
eighths
1 large onion, thinly sliced
1 clove garlic, finely chopped, if
desired
1 can (16 ounces) whole tomatoes
(undrained)
1 can (8 ounces) tomato sauce
½ medium green pepper, cut into
¼-inch strips
1 package (10 ounces) frozen peas

Shake flour, salt, monosodium glutamate and pepper in medium plastic or paper bag. Shake beef in flour mixture until coated.

Cook and stir beef in shortening in 12-inch skillet or Dutch oven over medium heat until brown. Add salt, potatoes, onion, garlic, tomatoes and tomato sauce; break up tomatoes with fork. Heat to boiling; reduce heat. Cover and simmer, stirring occasionally, 30 minutes. Stir in green pepper and peas. Heat to boiling; reduce heat. Cover and simmer until peas are tender, about 5 minutes.

6 servings.

Note: For thicker stew, shake ⅓ cup cold water and 2 tablespoons all-purpose flour in tightly covered container; gradually stir into stew. Heat to boiling, stirring constantly. Boil and stir 1 minute.

Jiffy Hamburger Stew

1 pound ground beef
2 cups diced potatoes
2 medium onions, chopped (about 1 cup)
2 teaspoons salt
⅛ teaspoon pepper
1 can (16 ounces) whole tomatoes, undrained
Snipped parsley

Cook and stir ground beef, potatoes and onion in 12-inch skillet until beef is brown and onion is tender. Drain fat. Stir in salt, pepper and tomatoes; break up tomatoes with fork. Heat to boiling; reduce heat. Cover and simmer, stirring occasionally, until potatoes are tender, 5 to 10 minutes. Garnish with parsley.

4 servings.

Meatball Stew

1 pound ground beef
½ cup dry bread crumbs
¼ cup milk
2 tablespoons finely chopped onion
1 teaspoon salt
½ teaspoon Worcestershire sauce
1 egg
Seasoning Mix (right)
1½ cups water
4 medium stalks celery, cut into ¼-inch slices (about 2 cups)
1 can (16 ounces) whole tomatoes, undrained
1 can (16 ounces) kidney beans, undrained

Mix ground beef, bread crumbs, milk, onion, salt, Worcestershire sauce and egg; shape into eighteen 1½-inch balls. Cook in Dutch oven over medium heat, turning occasionally, until brown, about 10 minutes. Stir in Seasoning Mix until meatballs are coated. Add water, celery, tomatoes and kidney beans. Heat to boiling, stirring frequently. Reduce heat; cover and simmer 30 minutes, stirring occasionally. Add additional water if necessary.

6 servings.

Seasoning Mix

¼ cup all-purpose flour
2 tablespoons instant minced onion
1 tablespoon instant beef bouillon
½ teaspoon salt
½ teaspoon garlic powder
½ teaspoon chili powder
½ teaspoon ground thyme
½ teaspoon dried basil leaves
⅛ teaspoon ground marjoram

Combine all ingredients.

Do-ahead Tip: Prepare several packages of Seasoning Mix and store in plastic bag or airtight container in a cool dry place. Use 1 Seasoning Mix package for each recipe of Meatball Stew (above) or Sausage Beer Stew (page 83).

Cabbage-Beef Stew with Dumplings

1 pound ground beef
1½ cups coarsely chopped cabbage
½ cup diced celery
2 medium onions, thinly sliced
1 cup water
1 teaspoon salt
1 to 2 teaspoons chili powder
¼ teaspoon pepper
1 can (16 ounces) stewed tomatoes
1 can (15½ ounces) kidney beans,
  undrained
Dumplings (right)

Cook and stir ground beef in Dutch oven until light brown; drain. Add cabbage, celery and onions; cook and stir until vegetables are light brown. Stir in water, salt, chili powder, pepper, tomatoes and kidney beans; break up tomatoes with fork. Heat to boiling; reduce heat. Cover and simmer 5 minutes.

Prepare Dumplings. Drop dough by spoonfuls onto hot beef and vegetables (do not drop directly into liquid). Cook uncovered over low heat 10 minutes. Cover and cook 10 minutes longer.

4 to 6 servings.

Dumplings

3 tablespoons shortening
1½ cups all-purpose flour
2 teaspoons baking powder
¾ teaspoon salt
¾ cup milk

Cut shortening into flour, baking powder and salt until mixture resembles fine crumbs. Stir in milk.

Barley-Beef Stew

1½ pounds ground beef
2 stalks celery, sliced (about 1 cup)
1 large onion, chopped (about
  1 cup)
2½ cups water
1 cup uncooked barley
1 tablespoon chili powder
1 teaspoon salt
¼ teaspoon pepper
1 can (28 ounces) whole tomatoes,
  undrained

Cook and stir ground beef, celery and onion in Dutch oven over medium heat until beef is brown; drain. Stir in remaining ingredients. Break up tomatoes with fork. Heat to boiling; reduce heat. Cover and simmer until barley is done and stew is desired consistency, about 1 hour.

6 servings.

Beef and Bulgur Stew

1½ **pounds ground beef**
1 **medium onion, chopped (about ½ cup)**
2 **cups water**
1 **cup uncooked cracked wheat (bulgur)**
1 **tablespoon snipped mint leaves or 1 teaspoon dried mint leaves**
1½ **teaspoons salt**
1 **teaspoon dried oregano leaves**
1 **small eggplant (about 1 pound), cut into 1-inch pieces**
¼ **cup grated Parmesan cheese**
2 **medium tomatoes, chopped (about 1½ cups)**

Cook and stir ground beef and onion in Dutch oven until beef is brown; drain. Stir in water, cracked wheat, mint, salt, oregano and eggplant. Heat to boiling; reduce heat. Cover and simmer, stirring occasionally, until wheat is tender, about 30 minutes (add small amount of water if necessary). Stir in cheese and tomatoes. Heat just until tomatoes are hot, about 5 minutes. Serve with additional cheese if desired.

8 servings.

Beef and Lentil Stew

1 **pound ground beef**
1 **medium onion, chopped (about ½ cup)**
1 **clove garlic, finely chopped**
3 **cups water**
¼ **cup red wine, if desired**
2 **tablespoons snipped parsley**
2 **teaspoons salt**
1 **teaspoon instant beef bouillon**
¼ **teaspoon pepper**
6 **ounces dried lentils (about 1 cup)**
1 **medium stalk celery, sliced (about ½ cup)**
1 **large carrot, sliced (about ¾ cup)**
1 **bay leaf**
1 **can (16 ounces) stewed tomatoes**
1 **can (4 ounces) mushroom stems and pieces, undrained**

Cook and stir ground beef, onion and garlic in Dutch oven until beef is brown; drain. Stir in remaining ingredients. Heat to boiling; reduce heat. Cover and simmer, stirring occasionally, until lentils are tender, about 40 minutes. Remove bay leaf.

6 servings.

Chili-roni

1 pound ground beef
2 medium onions, chopped (about
   1 cup)
1 medium green pepper, chopped
   (about 1 cup)
3½ ounces uncooked elbow
   macaroni (about 1 cup)
2 teaspoons chili powder
1 teaspoon salt
⅛ teaspoon cayenne pepper
⅛ teaspoon paprika
1 can (28 ounces) whole tomatoes,
   undrained
1 can (15½ ounces) kidney beans,
   undrained
1 can (8 ounces) tomato sauce

Cook and stir ground beef, onions and green pepper in 12-inch skillet until beef is brown and onions are tender; drain. Stir in remaining ingredients. Break up tomatoes with fork. Heat to boiling; reduce heat. Cover and simmer, stirring occasionally, until macaroni is tender, 20 to 30 minutes.

6 to 8 servings.

Chili con Carne: Omit elbow macaroni. Cook uncovered until desired consistency, about 45 minutes.

Chili with Rice

2 cups cubed cooked beef
2 cups mild salsa
1 cup water
1 tablespoon cornmeal
½ teaspoon ground cumin
¼ teaspoon crushed dried hot
   chilies, if desired
1 can (15 ounces) pinto beans
   Rice (right)

Heat beef, salsa, water, cornmeal, cumin and chilies to boiling, stirring frequently. Reduce heat; cover and simmer 30 minutes. Heat pinto beans until hot. Serve chili with pinto beans and Rice.

4 servings.

Rice

Heat 1⅓ cups water, ⅔ cup uncooked regular rice and ½ teaspoon salt to boiling, stirring once or twice; reduce heat. Cover and simmer 14 minutes. (Do not lift cover or stir.) Remove from heat. Fluff rice lightly with fork; cover and let steam 5 to 10 minutes.

Veal Stew

2-**pound veal round steak, ½ inch thick**
½ **cup all-purpose flour**
2 **teaspoons salt**
1 **teaspoon paprika**
¼ **teaspoon pepper**
¼ **cup olive or vegetable oil**
1 **cup dry white wine**
½ **cup water**
½ **teaspoon dried rosemary or thyme leaves**
8 **ounces tiny pearl onions, peeled (1½ cups)**
8 **to 10 tiny carrots or 4 medium carrots, cut into strips**
½ **teaspoon salt**
   Snipped parsley

Cut veal into serving pieces. Mix flour, 2 teaspoons salt, the paprika and pepper. Coat veal with flour mixture; pound until ¼ inch thick.

Cook veal in hot oil in 12-inch skillet until brown; drain. Add wine, water, rosemary, onions and carrots. Sprinkle with ½ teaspoon salt. Heat to boiling; reduce heat. Cover and simmer until veal and vegetables are tender, about 45 minutes. (Add small amount of water if necessary.) Place veal and vegetables on platter; pour pan juices on top. Sprinkle with parsley.

8 servings.

Veal Stew with Cornmeal Dumplings

2 slices lean salt pork
1½ pounds veal boneless shoulder, cut into 1-inch pieces
4 cups tomato juice
1 teaspoon salt
2 or 3 dashes red pepper sauce
Dash of pepper
1 cup diced potatoes
1 medium stalk celery, chopped (about ½ cup)
1 medium onion, chopped (about ½ cup)
Cornmeal Dumplings (right)

Fry salt pork in Dutch oven until crisp. Remove with slotted spoon; drain and reserve. Brown veal slowly in pork fat over low heat, about 30 minutes. Remove excess fat. Crumble salt pork. Add salt pork, tomato juice, salt, pepper sauce and pepper to veal. Cover and simmer 1 hour. Add potatoes, celery and onion. Cover and simmer until vegetables are crisp-tender, about 30 minutes. (Add additional ½ to 1 cup tomato juice if necessary.)

Prepare Cornmeal Dumplings. Drop dough by spoonfuls onto hot veal or vegetables (do not drop directly into liquid). Cook uncovered over low heat 10 minutes. Cover and cook 10 minutes longer.

Cornmeal Dumplings

1½ cups buttermilk baking mix
½ cup yellow cornmeal
2 teaspoons dried parsley flakes
¾ cup milk

Mix baking mix, cornmeal, parsley flakes and milk until soft dough forms.

Pork and Sauerkraut Stew

4 slices bacon
2 pounds pork boneless Boston shoulder
1 tablespoon paprika
2 to 3 teaspoons caraway seed
1 teaspoon salt
1 clove garlic, finely chopped
1½ cups water
10 small new potatoes (about 1 pound)
4 medium onions, sliced
1 can (16 ounces) sauerkraut, drained
½ teaspoon salt
Snipped parsley
¾ cup dairy sour cream

Fry bacon in Dutch oven over medium heat until crisp. Remove bacon; drain and reserve. Trim excess fat from pork shoulder; cut pork into 1-inch pieces. Brown pork in bacon fat; drain. Sprinkle pork with paprika, caraway seed, 1 teaspoon salt and the garlic. Stir in water, potatoes, onions and sauerkraut. Sprinkle with ½ teaspoon salt. Heat to boiling; reduce heat. Cover and simmer until pork is tender, about 1 hour.

Crumble bacon; sprinkle bacon and parsley over pork mixture. Serve with sour cream.

6 servings.

Pork-Vegetable Stew

4 slices bacon, cut into ½-inch pieces
1½ pounds pork boneless shoulder, cut into 1-inch pieces
½ cup water
1 teaspoon salt
1 teaspoon dried rosemary leaves
¼ teaspoon pepper
⅛ teaspoon ground cloves
1 large onion, chopped (about 1 cup)
2 medium cloves garlic, crushed
1 can (10¾ ounces) condensed chicken broth
2 medium rutabagas, cut into 1-inch pieces (about 3 cups)
1 package (10 ounces) frozen baby Brussels sprouts
1 tablespoon cornstarch
2 tablespoons cold water

Fry bacon in Dutch oven over medium heat until crisp. Remove bacon; drain and reserve. Pour off all but 2 tablespoons bacon fat. Cook pork in bacon fat, stirring occasionally, until brown. Stir in water, salt, rosemary, pepper, cloves, onion, garlic and broth. Heat to boiling; reduce heat. Cover and simmer 30 minutes.

Add rutabagas. Heat to boiling; reduce heat. Cover and simmer 20 minutes. Rinse Brussels sprouts under running cold water to separate; drain. Stir Brussels sprouts and bacon into pork mixture. Cover and simmer until Brussels sprouts are done, about 10 minutes. Mix cornstarch and 2 tablespoons cold water; gradually stir into pork mixture. Heat to boiling, stirring constantly. Boil and stir 1 minute.

6 servings.

Sausage Beer Stew

1½ pounds Polish sausage or
    bratwurst, cut into ½-inch
    pieces
1 can or bottle (12 ounces) beer
  Seasoning Mix (page 76)
6 carrots, cut into 1-inch pieces
6 new potatoes, cut into ½-inch
    pieces
1 medium onion, thinly sliced

Cook sausage in Dutch oven over medium heat, stirring frequently, until brown, about 8 minutes. Stir in Seasoning Mix until sausage is coated. Add enough water to beer to measure 2 cups; pour onto sausage. Stir in carrots, potatoes and onion. Heat to boiling, stirring constantly; reduce heat. Cover and simmer until vegetables are tender, about 45 minutes. (Add small amount of water if necessary.)

6 servings.

Mixed Skillet Dinner

1 pound bulk pork sausage
1 pound ground lamb
1 cup dry bread crumbs
1 cup finely chopped onion
¼ cup snipped parsley
½ teaspoon salt
1 egg
1 teaspoon salt
¼ teaspoon pepper
¼ teaspoon dried rosemary leaves
¼ teaspoon dried oregano leaves
1 can (6 ounces) cocktail vegetable
    juice
½ head cabbage, shredded
1 package (10 ounces) frozen peas
    and carrots, broken apart

Mix pork, lamb, bread crumbs, onion, parsley, ½ teaspoon salt and the egg. Shape into 1½-inch balls. Cook in 12-inch skillet over medium heat, turning occasionally, until brown, about 20 minutes; drain. Stir in 1 teaspoon salt, the pepper, rosemary, oregano and vegetable juice. Push meatballs to one side of skillet; add cabbage and peas. Heat to boiling; reduce heat. Cover and simmer 15 minutes, stirring occasionally.

6 servings.

Brunswick-style Stew

1 pound bulk pork sausage
2 turkey legs (about 3 pounds)
1 cup water
1 teaspoon dried basil leaves
½ teaspoon salt
½ teaspoon red pepper sauce
2 medium stalks celery, sliced
    (about 1 cup)
1 large onion, sliced
1 bay leaf
1 can (16 ounces) whole tomatoes,
    undrained
1 package (10 ounces) frozen whole
    kernel corn
1 package (10 ounces) frozen baby
    lima beans
2 tablespoons snipped parsley

Cook and stir sausage in Dutch oven until brown. Remove with slotted spoon and drain; reserve. Pour off all but 1 tablespoon fat. Cook turkey legs in fat, turning occasionally, until golden brown. Add sausage, water, basil, salt, pepper sauce, celery, onion and bay leaf. Heat to boiling; reduce heat. Cover and simmer until turkey is done, 2 to 2½ hours.

Remove turkey; cool slightly. Remove turkey from bones and skin; cut turkey into bite-size pieces. Return turkey to Dutch oven; add tomatoes, corn and lima beans. Break up tomatoes with fork. Heat to boiling; reduce heat. Cover and simmer until vegetables are tender, about 10 minutes. Sprinkle with parsley.

8 servings.

Lamb and Green Bean Stew

1½ pounds lamb boneless shoulder
1 tablespoon vegetable oil
½ cup water
1 teaspoon salt
1 clove garlic, chopped
½ teaspoon salt
¼ teaspoon dried thyme leaves
⅛ to ¼ teaspoon crushed red
   peppers
1 pound green beans, cut
   diagonally into 1-inch pieces
   (about 4 cups)
2 potatoes, cut into 1-inch pieces
1 medium onion, sliced

Trim fat from lamb; cut lamb into ¾-inch pieces. Heat oil in Dutch oven or 12-inch skillet until hot. Cook and stir lamb in oil over medium heat until brown, about 10 minutes. Add water, 1 teaspoon salt and the garlic. Cover and simmer over low heat 40 minutes. Skim fat.

Stir in ½ teaspoon salt, the thyme, red peppers, beans, potatoes and onion. (Add small amount of water if necessary. There should be just enough liquid to steam the vegetables and prevent scorching.) Heat to boiling; reduce heat. Cover and simmer, stirring occasionally, until lamb and vegetables are tender, about 30 minutes. Serve with hot cooked rice if desired.

4 servings.

Springtime Skillet Stew

1½ pounds lamb boneless shoulder
1 tablespoon shortening
2 medium onions, chopped (about
   1 cup)
2 cups Beef Broth (page 6)
½ teaspoon salt
¼ teaspoon celery seed
¼ teaspoon dried marjoram leaves
⅛ teaspoon dried thyme leaves
¼ teaspoon pepper
3 medium potatoes, thinly sliced
1 package (10 ounces) frozen green
   peas, broken apart

Trim fat from lamb; cut lamb into 2-inch pieces. Heat shortening in 12-inch skillet or Dutch oven until hot. Cook and stir lamb in shortening over medium heat until brown; drain. Add onions. Cook and stir until tender. Pour broth over lamb and onions. Heat to boiling; reduce heat. Cover and simmer 2 hours.

Stir in salt, celery seed, marjoram, thyme, pepper and potatoes. Heat to boiling; reduce heat. Cover and simmer 30 minutes. Skim fat. Stir in peas. Cover and cook 10 minutes.

4 servings.

Irish Stew

2 pounds lamb boneless neck or
   shoulder
6 medium potatoes (about
   2 pounds)
3 medium onions, sliced
2 teaspoons salt
¼ teaspoon pepper
2 cups water
   Snipped parsley

Trim fat from lamb; cut lamb into 1-inch pieces. Cut potatoes into ½-inch slices. Layer half each of the lamb, potatoes and onions in Dutch oven; sprinkle with half each of the salt and pepper. Repeat. Add water.

Heat to boiling; reduce heat. Cover and simmer until lamb is tender, 1½ to 2 hours. Skim fat. Sprinkle with parsley. Serve in bowls with pickled red cabbage if desired.

6 servings.

Couscous

2 tablespoons olive or vegetable oil
2½- to 3-pound broiler-fryer
    chicken, cut up
1 cup water
2 teaspoons ground coriander
1½ teaspoons salt
1 teaspoon instant chicken
    bouillon
¼ teaspoon cayenne pepper
¼ teaspoon ground turmeric
4 small carrots, cut into 2-inch
    pieces
2 medium onions, sliced
2 medium turnips, cut into
    fourths
2 cloves garlic, finely chopped
3 zucchini, cut into ¼-inch slices
1 can (about 16 ounces) garbanzo
    beans, drained
    Couscous (right)

Heat oil in Dutch oven until hot. Cook chicken in oil over medium heat until brown, about 15 minutes. Drain fat from Dutch oven. Add water, coriander, salt, bouillon (dry), cayenne pepper, turmeric, carrots, onions, turnips and garlic. Heat to boiling; reduce heat. Cover and simmer 30 minutes.

Add zucchini to chicken mixture. Cover and cook until thickest pieces of chicken are done and vegetables are tender, about 10 minutes. Add beans; heat 5 minutes.

Prepare Couscous. Mound on center of heated platter; arrange chicken and vegetables around Couscous.

6 or 7 servings.

Couscous

1⅓ cups couscous (semolina wheat
    cereal)
¾ cup raisins
½ teaspoon salt
1 cup boiling water
½ cup margarine or butter
½ teaspoon ground turmeric

Mix couscous, raisins and salt in 2-quart bowl; stir in boiling water. Let stand until all water is absorbed, 2 to 3 minutes. Heat margarine in 10-inch skillet until melted; stir in couscous and turmeric. Cook over medium heat, stirring occasionally, 4 minutes.

Country Captain

½ cup all-purpose flour
1 teaspoon salt
¼ teaspoon pepper
2½- to 3-pound broiler-fryer
    chicken, cut up
¼ cup vegetable oil
1½ teaspoons curry powder
½ teaspoon dried thyme leaves
¼ teaspoon salt
1 large onion, chopped
1 green pepper, chopped
1 clove garlic, finely chopped, or
    ⅛ teaspoon garlic powder
1 can (16 ounces) whole tomatoes,
    undrained
¼ cup currants or raisins
⅓ cup toasted slivered blanched
    almonds
    Rice (right)

Heat oven to 350°. Mix flour, 1 teaspoon salt and the pepper; coat chicken. Heat oil in 10-inch skillet until hot. Cook chicken in oil over medium heat until brown, 15 to 20 minutes. Place chicken in ungreased 2½-quart casserole. Drain fat from skillet.

Add curry powder, thyme, ¼ teaspoon salt, the onion, green pepper, garlic and tomatoes to skillet. Break up tomatoes with fork. Heat to boiling, stirring frequently to loosen brown particles from skillet. Pour over chicken. Cover and bake until thickest pieces of chicken are done, about 40 minutes. Skim fat if necessary; add currants. Bake 5 minutes. Sprinkle with almonds. Serve with Rice. Serve with grated fresh coconut and chutney if desired.

4 servings.

Rice

Heat 2 cups water, 1 cup uncooked regular rice and 1 teaspoon salt to boiling, stirring once or twice; reduce heat. Cover and simmer 14 minutes. (Do not lift cover or stir.) Remove from heat. Fluff rice lightly with fork; cover and let steam 5 to 10 minutes.

Coq au Vin

2½- to 3-pound broiler-fryer chicken
½ cup all-purpose flour
1 teaspoon salt
¼ teaspoon pepper
8 slices bacon
8 small onions
8 ounces mushrooms, sliced
   (about 3 cups)
1 cup Chicken Broth (page 8)
1 cup dry red wine
½ teaspoon salt
4 carrots, cut into halves
1 clove garlic, crushed
   Bouquet garni*

Cut chicken into pieces; cut each breast half into halves. Mix flour, 1 teaspoon salt and the pepper; coat chicken. Fry bacon in 12-inch skillet until crisp. Remove with slotted spoon and drain; reserve. Cook chicken in bacon fat until brown, about 15 minutes.

Push chicken to one side; add onions and mushrooms. Cook and stir until mushrooms are tender. Drain fat from skillet. Crumble bacon and stir into vegetables with the remaining ingredients. Cover and simmer until thickest pieces of chicken are done, about 35 minutes. Remove bouquet garni; skim fat. Sprinkle chicken with snipped parsley if desired.

6 to 7 servings.

*Tie ½ teaspoon dried thyme leaves, 2 large sprigs parsley and 1 bay leaf in cheesecloth bag or place in tea ball.

Chicken and Rice Stew

2½- to 3-pound broiler-fryer
   chicken, cut up
2 teaspoons salt
1 teaspoon dried oregano leaves
½ teaspoon ground coriander
¼ teaspoon pepper
2 cups water
1 medium onion, chopped (about
   ½ cup)
1 clove garlic, crushed
1 can (16 ounces) stewed
   tomatoes
1 cup uncooked regular rice
1 package (10 ounces) frozen
   green peas
1 medium green pepper, chopped,
   (about 1 cup)
½ cup cubed fully cooked smoked
   ham (about 2 ounces)
⅓ cup pitted small green olives
1 tablespoon capers
   Grated Parmesan cheese

Place chicken in 12-inch skillet or Dutch oven. Sprinkle with salt, oregano, coriander and pepper. Add water, onion, garlic and tomatoes. Heat to boiling; reduce heat. Cover and simmer 30 minutes.

Stir rice into liquid. Cover and simmer until thickest pieces of chicken are done, about 20 minutes. Rinse frozen peas under running cold water to separate; drain. Add peas, green pepper, ham, olives, capers and 1 tablespoon caper liquid to chicken. Cover and simmer 5 minutes. Serve with cheese.

8 servings.

Kentucky Burgoo

4- to 5-pound stewing chicken, cut
    up
1 pound beef stew meat, cut into
    2-inch pieces
1 pound veal boneless shoulder,
    cut into 2-inch pieces
2 tablespoons salt
1½ teaspoons dry mustard
1 teaspoon chili powder
1 teaspoon pepper
¼ teaspoon red pepper sauce
⅛ teaspoon cayenne pepper
6 small potatoes (about 1 pound),
    cut into halves
6 small onions (about 1 pound),
    cut into halves
6 medium stalks celery, chopped
    (about 3 cups)
4 medium carrots, sliced (about
    2 cups)
2 medium green peppers, chopped
    (about 2 cups)
1 can (16 ounces) cut okra, or
    1 package (10 ounces) frozen
    okra, broken apart
1 can (16 ounces) whole kernel
    corn, undrained
1 can (16 ounces) tomatoes,
    undrained
1 can (10½ ounces) tomato puree
1 package (10 ounces) frozen lima
    beans, broken apart
½ cup snipped parsley

Remove any excess fat from chicken. Place chicken, beef and veal in Dutch oven. Add water just to cover meat (10 to 12 cups). Cover and cook over low heat until done, 2 to 3 hours. Remove meat from Dutch oven; skim excess fat from broth. Remove chicken from bones and skin. Cut chicken into bite-size pieces. Return meat to broth; add remaining ingredients except parsley. Break up tomatoes with fork. Heat to boiling; reduce heat. Simmer uncovered until flavors are blended, 2½ to 3 hours. Just before serving, stir in parsley.

About 20 servings.

Handling Raw Chicken

Raw chicken should be handled properly. Here are a few tips to remember:
- When cutting up raw poultry and meat, choose a plastic cutting surface rather than a wooden board. You'll find the plastic one less porous and easier to clean.
- After handling raw chicken, wash your hands carefully before touching other foods that are not going to be cooked—salad fixings, for example.
- Be sure to thoroughly clean the cutting surface, counter top and all utensils used in the preparation of the chicken. Wooden cutting boards can be washed with a solution of 1 teaspoon chlorine bleach and ½ teaspoon vinegar to 2 quarts water.

Oyster Stew

2½ cups Chicken Broth (page 8)
2 tablespoons soy sauce
¼ teaspoon grated gingerroot
1 pint shucked select or large
   oysters
2 cups chopped Chinese cabbage
8 ounces sliced mushrooms
½ cup bean sprouts*
4 green onions with tops, cut into
   1-inch pieces

Heat Chicken Broth, soy sauce and gingerroot to boiling in 3-quart saucepan. Add oysters (with liquid), cabbage, mushrooms and bean sprouts. Heat to boiling; reduce heat. Cover and simmer until cabbage is crisp-tender, about 2 minutes. Garnish each serving with green onions.

4 servings.

*Pea pods can be substituted for the bean sprouts.

Bouillabaisse

2 medium onions, chopped (about
   1 cup)
¼ cup chopped carrot
1 clove garlic, finely chopped
½ cup vegetable oil
3 pounds frozen fish fillets, thawed
   and cut into 3-inch pieces
8 cups water
2 bay leaves
1 can (16 ounces) whole tomatoes,
   undrained
½ cup chopped pimiento
¼ cup snipped parsley
1 tablespoon salt
1 tablespoon lemon juice
½ teaspoon saffron
   Dash of pepper
6 frozen lobster tails, thawed and
   cut lengthwise into halves
1 pound fresh or frozen raw shrimp,
   shelled and deveined
1 can (10½ ounces) condensed beef
   broth
1 can (10 ounces) whole clams (with
   liquid)

Cook and stir onions, carrot and garlic in oil in Dutch oven until onion is tender, about 10 minutes. Add fish fillets, water, bay leaves and tomatoes; break up tomatoes with fork. Heat to boiling; reduce heat. Cover and simmer 30 minutes. Stir in remaining ingredients; cover and simmer 30 minutes. Remove bay leaves.

About 18 servings.

Cioppino

3 pounds dressed firm saltwater fish (sea bass, halibut, haddock, turbot)
1 live Dungeness crab
1 pound large fresh or frozen raw shrimp
12 clams, oysters or mussels (or combination)
2 large onions, chopped (about 2 cups)
1 medium green pepper, chopped (about 1 cup)
¼ cup olive oil
1 to 2 teaspoons salt
½ teaspoon dried basil leaves
⅛ teaspoon pepper
2 cloves garlic, finely chopped
1 bay leaf
2 cups tomato juice
1 can (28 ounces) whole tomatoes, undrained
2 cups dry red wine
Snipped parsley

Cut fish into serving pieces. Cook and crack crab. Peel and devein shrimp. Steam clams to open; remove top shells and reserve liquid. Place fish and crab in 8-quart Dutch oven; reserve shrimp and clams.

Cook and stir onions and green pepper in oil in 3-quart saucepan until onions are tender. Stir in reserved clam liquid, salt, basil, pepper, garlic, bay leaf, tomato juice and tomatoes; break up tomatoes with fork. Heat to boiling; reduce heat. Simmer uncovered 10 minutes. Stir in wine; pour over fish and crab. Heat to boiling; reduce heat. Cover and simmer 20 minutes. Add shrimp. Cover and simmer 5 minutes. Arrange clams on the half shells on top. Cover and simmer 3 minutes. Remove bay leaf. Sprinkle with parsley.

18 to 20 servings.

Cooking a Hard-shell Crab

To cook a live crab, use tongs to grasp the crab behind the back fins; plunge it headfirst into a kettle or large pot of boiling salted or seasoned water. Simmer uncovered for about 20 minutes. Remove cooked crab with tongs and place on a plate. With your hands, crack the crab's body into halves or cut with a sharp knife. Remove meat from crab with a meat pick or small knife.

Chili Fish Stew

1 medium onion, thinly sliced
2 large cloves garlic, crushed
2 tablespoons olive or vegetable oil
1 tablespoon chili powder
3 cups Chicken Broth (page 8)
1 can (4 ounces) chopped green
    chilies, undrained
1 teaspoon salt
4 medium tomatoes, coarsely
    chopped (about 3 cups)
1 medium green pepper, chopped
    (about 1 cup)
1 pound frozen fish fillets,
    partially thawed and cut into
    1-inch pieces
1 can (6½ ounces) crabmeat,
    drained and cartilage
    removed, or 1 can (4¼ ounces)
    tiny shrimp, rinsed and
    drained
1½ cups plain yogurt
    Snipped cilantro or parsley

Cook and stir onion and garlic in oil in Dutch oven until onion is tender, about 5 minutes. Add chili powder; cook and stir 2 minutes. Add Chicken Broth and green chilies. Heat to boiling; reduce heat. Cover and simmer 20 minutes.

Stir in salt, tomatoes, green pepper, fish and crabmeat. Heat to boiling; reduce heat. Cover and simmer until fish flakes easily with fork, about 3 minutes. Gradually stir in yogurt; heat just until hot (do not boil). Sprinkle with cilantro.

9 servings.

For ease in cutting into pieces, partially thaw the frozen fish fillets.

Fish Stew with Vegetables

4 cups water
1 cup uncooked regular rice
1 tablespoon salt
½ teaspoon cayenne pepper
3 carrots, thinly sliced
1 onion, thinly sliced
1 can (15 ounces) tomato sauce
1 package (10 ounces) frozen okra pods
1 package (10 ounces) frozen green beans
3 cups sliced cabbage
1½ pounds catfish, perch, bass or trout fillets, cut into serving pieces

Heat water, rice, salt, cayenne pepper, carrots, onion and tomato sauce in Dutch oven to boiling; reduce heat. Cover and cook 10 minutes.

Rinse okra and green beans under running cold water to separate; drain. Cut okra lengthwise into halves. Add okra, green beans, cabbage and fish to Dutch oven. Heat to boiling; reduce heat. Cover and cook until fish flakes easily with fork and vegetables are tender, 10 to 12 minutes.

8 servings.

Budget Bouillabaisse

1 medium onion, chopped (about ½ cup)
1 small stalk celery, chopped (about ½ cup)
1 tablespoon vegetable oil
1 tablespoon snipped parsley
½ teaspoon lemon juice
¼ teaspoon salt
¼ teaspoon dried thyme leaves
⅛ teaspoon dried oregano leaves
⅛ teaspoon fennel seed
1 clove garlic, finely chopped
1 small bay leaf
  Dash of cayenne pepper
1 can (28 ounces) whole tomatoes, undrained
2 cans (10¾ ounces each) condensed chicken broth
½ cup cold water
2 tablespoons cornstarch
1 pound frozen cod, partially thawed and cut into 1-inch pieces

Cook and stir onion and celery in oil in 3-quart saucepan over medium heat until onion is tender, about 4 minutes. Stir in parsley, lemon juice, salt, thyme, oregano, fennel seed, garlic, bay leaf, cayenne pepper and tomatoes. Heat to boiling; reduce heat. Simmer uncovered 15 minutes. Add broth. Stir water into cornstarch; stir into broth mixture. Cook, stirring constantly, until mixture thickens and boils. Stir in cod. Simmer uncovered until cod flakes easily with fork, about 10 minutes. Sprinkle with salt and pepper if desired.

7 servings.

Bean and Hominy Stew

1 package (10 ounces) frozen sliced okra, rinsed and drained
1 can (30 ounces) kidney beans, drained
1 can (20 ounces) hominy, drained
1 can (16 ounces) whole tomatoes, undrained
2 medium stalks celery, thinly sliced (about 1 cup)
1 tablespoon Worcestershire sauce
½ teaspoon salt
⅛ teaspoon dried dill weed
1½ cups shredded cheese (about 6 ounces)
2 tablespoons imitation bacon

Rinse frozen okra under running cold water to separate; drain. Mix okra, beans, hominy, tomatoes, celery, Worcestershire sauce, salt and dill weed in ungreased 2-quart casserole; break up tomatoes with fork. Sprinkle with cheese. Cook uncovered in 350° oven until hot and cheese is melted, about 30 minutes. Sprinkle with imitation bacon. Serve with French bread if desired.

6 servings.

Lentil and Vegetable Stew

3 cups Beef Broth (page 6)
8 ounces dried lentils (about 1¼ cups)
1 tablespoon finely snipped parsley
1 teaspoon salt
1 teaspoon ground cumin
2 medium potatoes, cut into 1-inch cubes (about 2 cups)
1 medium onion, chopped (about ½ cup)
1 medium stalk celery, chopped (about ½ cup)
2 cloves garlic, finely chopped
2 medium zucchini, cut into ½-inch slices (about 4 cups)
Lemon wedges

Heat Beef Broth and lentils to boiling in Dutch oven; reduce heat. Cover and cook until lentils are almost tender, about 30 minutes.

Stir in parsley, salt, cumin, potatoes, onion, celery and garlic. Cover and cook until potatoes are tender, about 20 minutes. Stir in zucchini; cover and cook until zucchini is tender, 10 to 15 minutes. Serve with lemon wedges.

4 or 5 servings.

Index